Mint Tea

Charity, Creation, and Other Short Stories to Warm the Heart

Volume 3

BY IMAN ABDALLAH AL-QAISI

Illustrator
Nadia Yousef

Translators
Maha Mustafa
Hadia Mahmoud

Copy Editors
Susan (Sumaiya) T. Gavell
Maha Ezzeddine

Layout and Graphics

pandaUX.studio.com
Thought. Action. Interaction.

Acknowledgments

"If you express gratitude, I shall certainly give you more ..."

[Ibrahim:7]

The Prophet (pbuh) said: "He has not thanked God who has not thanked people." Narrated by Abu Dawud

We hope to express our deepest gratitude and appreciation to all of those who made this book possible, all Praise be to God. Your tireless efforts and concern for this project was truly paramount for its success. We pray that you will find your reward with God that will far surpass your greatest imagination. Special thanks to:

Fatma Almaery, Freda Shamma, Allison Carpenter, Afraa Jasim, Abdullah Khatib, Hanan Abu Salah, Dima Almeniawi and Fedaa Jasim.

Introduction

It is often said that a fireplace without books is incomplete. As a fireplace warms the body, books warm the soul. A Cup of Mint Tea is just that book. With stories that will inspire and educate, Iman Al-Qaisi has brought together a collection of short stories that are certainly going to have children asking, "One more read, please!"

Imām Suhaib Webb

CONTENTS

"Trials are presented to the hearts, like straws sewn into a woven mat, one after another. Upon any heart that is affected by evil trials, a black dot will be engraved. Upon any heart that averts evil trials, a white dot will be engraved. The hearts will therefore become two categories: white, just like the barren rock; no trial shall ever harm this category as long as the heavens and the earth still exist. Another category is black, just as the cup that is overturned, for this heart does not recognize righteousness or renounce evil."

Prophet Muhammad (PBUH)
Narrated by Muslim

— 1 —

Piety and the Heart

The Wise Carpenter Luqman [1]

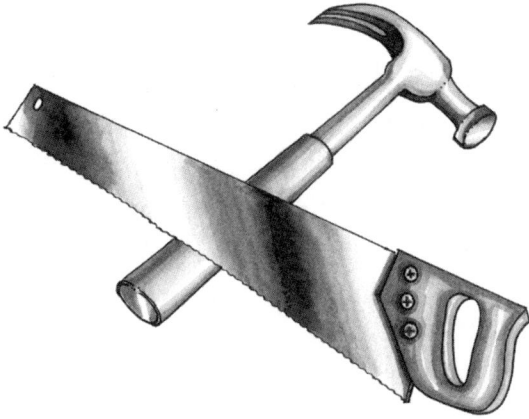

Luqman was an Abyssinian servant who worked as a carpenter. One day, his master instructed him to slaughter a sheep. So Luqman dutifully prepared the animal and performed the slaughter. After he had completed the task, his master made a strange request.

"Bring me the two purest parts of the sheep!"

Luqman thought for a moment before he carried out the instructions. He carefully separated the tongue and the heart, and presented them to his master as the two purest parts of the animal.

A few days later, Luqman was told again to slaughter a

---

[1] Dalil Al-Sa'ileen, pg. 115, by Anas Ismail Abu Dawud, story narrated by Khalid Al-Rabi'i.

sheep. No sooner did he prepare the animal and perform the slaughter than his master made another strange request.

"Bring the two filthiest parts of the sheep!"

Luqman thought about this, and, after a few moments, he presented his master with the exact same organs: the tongue and the heart. The master was intrigued by these choices. Puzzled, he asked Luqman, "How can the tongue and the heart be both the purest and filthiest parts?"

Luqman responded wisely, "Nothing in the body is more pure than the tongue and the heart when they have been kept pure, and nothing is filthier than the two when they have been corrupted."

Lessons Learned:

1. Don't Judge a Book by Its Cover

Luqman was merely a humble servant who worked as a carpenter. If judged simply by his status or outward appearance, no one would have assumed him to be a man of great wisdom and beneficial knowledge from whom others might learn a great deal. It is important always to look at a person's character and behavior, and to avoid judging people using superficial gauges.

2. A Pure Heart Can Lead to Paradise

The Prophet (pbuh) [2] said, "In the body there is a piece of flesh. If it is sound, the whole body is sound, and if it is corrupt, the whole body is corrupt. Verily it is the heart." [3]

When keeping the heart pure, a balanced love and fear of God (*taqwa*), patience, compassion and so many other beautiful qualities can be achieved. The heart is what moves the eyes to shed tears during the remembrance of God, the hand to give generously for the sake of God, the feet to stand during the darkest hours of the night in front of God in prayer, and the limbs to hasten to worship and do good. The driving force behind every single action is the heart, and acts of worship will be accepted based on the purity of the intentions.

3. A Corrupt Heart Is Perilous

When a heart is corrupted with feelings of anger, jealousy, envy, hatred, and bitterness, it leads to harmful actions. A corrupted heart is the culprit

---

[2] Acronym for "peace be upon him." Common Islamic etiquette dictates prayers of peace to be made for the Prophet Muhammad (pbuh) at every written or spoken mention of his beloved name.

[3] Narrated by Bukhari and Muslim.

behind behavior such as laziness in performing prayers, selfishness, envy and even murder. Early scholars tried to find a practical prescription for ailing hearts. They found that making a habit of praying, giving charity, reciting the holy Quran, and supplicating (*duaa*) could be an effective solution. Watch the heart very carefully, for it can lead to the greatest height in the Hereafter or to unbelievable danger and loss.

4. A Pure Tongue Beautifies and Illuminates

A clean tongue and pure speech makes the entire face radiant. A person with such good speech pleases God through supplication, remembrance, and recitation of the Quran. When speaking kind, encouraging words and forgiving faults, a person is gaining reward while also bringing happiness to everyone around. Be among the people who choose only the purest speech, and grow closer to God through the sweetest words.

5. A Foul Tongue Leads to Hardship and Pain

A foul tongue repels others and darkens the heart. When people lie, backbite, slander, brag, mock, defame, and curse they are using their tongue to create hardship and sadness. If persistent, these actions warrant God's anger. The Prophet (pbuh) said: "Whoever believes in God and the Last Day, let him speak goodness or be silent." [4]

6. God-Consciousness Affects the Tongue and the Heart

God-consciousness (*taqwa*) means to place a barrier between oneself and anything that is unpleasing to God. Actions originate from the heart and some are then translated into action by the tongue. If both the tongue and the heart are purified, they can elevate a

---

[4] Narrated by Muslim.

person to the highest levels of worship and take that person to Paradise. The Prophet (pbuh) was asked, "What are the things that are most likely to help a person enter Paradise?" The Prophet (pbuh) answered, "God-consciousness and excellent character." [5]

[5] Narrated by Ahmed, Ibn Majah, and Tirmidhi.

It is upon you to fear God (have taqwa) when you are heedless.
Provision will come from where you do not expect.

How do you fear poverty when God is the Provider?
Indeed, He provides for the birds and the fish in the sea.

And whoever thinks that provision comes with strength.
Then birds would not have anything to eat next to the eagles.

Abandon your worldly attachments, because you never know.
When night falls whether you will live until the morning.

Imam Al-Shafi

— 2 —

Reaching God Through Virtuous Deeds
The Three Men and the Cave[6]

One day, three men set out on a distant journey. They traveled until the day grew long and night began to fall. The travelers decided to take shelter for the night in a mountain cave. During the night, a boulder high upon the mountain's peak came crashing down. It tumbled down the mountainside and became lodged in the opening of the cave in which the three men were resting.

The travelers woke from their sleep, frantic and alarmed. The only exit had been sealed and there was no other escape. Unable to budge the heavy boulder, the trapped men faced one another in the dark to discuss a solution. Together they reached a unanimous conclusion: there was no way out except by turning to God.

---

[6] Hadith of the Prophet Muhammad (pbuh), narrated by Bukhari and Muslim.

The men prayed to God fervently. Desperate for God's help, each man made his most sincere supplication. Each recalled the most virtuous and sincere deed he had ever done for the sake of God alone.

The first man recalled his kindness towards his parents. He said, "Oh God! I took care of my elderly parents and my own small children at the same time. When I returned home every evening from milking the camels, I always let my parents drink from the milk before myself or my children.

"One night, I returned home late, and my parents had already gone to bed. I feared waking them from their sleep and disturbing their rest, so I waited at their bedside with their cup of milk in case they woke up hungry during the night. Even though my children wished for the milk, I waited beside my parents' bed until morning so that I could offer them the first drink of milk.

"O God! If you judge that I acted sincerely seeking Your pleasure alone, then please make a way out of this cave for us!" God answered his prayer. The boulder shifted slightly and forced a small opening. A breezy gust of fresh air reached the trapped men.

The second man began his supplication, remembering a moment of reverence and fear of disobeying God.

"Dear God, I had a cousin whom I loved very much. I shared my feelings with her, but she turned me down. One day, she was in great need of money, so I gave her the amount she needed to ease her burden. I continued my advances and tried once again to persuade her to show some interest in me. Because I had helped her and she felt indebted to me, she hesitantly agreed. But then, as I began to approach her, she warned, 'Oh servant of God, fear God! Do not come near me except in the way God allows!' Her words struck me, and I immediately left. Oh God, if you consider that I acted for only Your sake, then give us relief!" Just as he concluded his prayer, the boulder shifted even more and the opening grew wider.

The last man recalled his fairness and trustworthiness. The man said, "Oh God, I employed many laborers, and each would receive his compensation upon completion of his work. But one worker left without collecting his wages. A long time passed before the laborer returned to me and requested his payment. I told him, 'I was worried the value of your wages would diminish while you were away, so I invested the amount for you. All you see here of camels, cows, and sheep, belongs to you.'

"The laborer stared at the livestock and replied in disbelief, 'Do not tease me.'

"I assured him, 'I am not teasing you; it is true. So take your property, God bless you in it!'

"Oh God, if You deem that I did so to seek only Your pleasure, then free us from this hardship!"

God answered his prayer and rewarded his honesty and sincerity. The boulder rolled away and left the entrance of the cave clear for them to depart. The three men walked freely out of the cave, thanking God all the while.

Lessons Learned:

1. **Good Deeds Come to the Rescue**

   Acts of worship brighten the face, illuminate the heart, multiply the provision, strengthen the body, and place love in the hearts of people. Conversely, sins bring gloom to the face, blacken the heart, weaken the body, decrease the provision, and sow hatred in the hearts of people.

2. **God Is Present in Times of Hardship**

   The travelers drew close to God by doing good deeds in times of ease, so God eased their struggles during a time of hardship. The Prophet (pbuh) advised, "Be mindful of God, and you will find him with you. Know God during times of ease, and He will know you during times of hardship." [6] Always stay close to God in order to be granted His protection in this world and in the Hereafter.

3. **Piety Is Easier When Deeds Are Secret**

   Many do work for the sake of God, but good deeds may sometimes become tainted when done for show and recognition. Be mindful to keep at least some deeds secret so that only God witnesses the acts and intentions remain pure. That way, one can someday raise his or her hands and say, "My Lord, I come to You with these deeds that only You know." God might then ease one's hardships and difficulty, and grant tremendous rewards.

4. **Honoring Parents Is One of the Best Deeds**

   The Prophet (pbuh) taught us how to love, respect, honor, and provide for our parents. One should strive

---

[7] Narrated by Tirmidhi.

11

to never stand in the way of their comfort or make them feel burdensome. Be a son or daughter who thinks of thoughtful ways to delight his or her parents. There are great blessings in this world and the next for those who excel in honoring their parents.

5. Piety Prevents Falling into Forbidden Acts

Remembering that God is always watching is a form of piety (*taqwa*) and keeps a person away from sin and impurity. When a person forgets that God is watching, it is easy to make decisions that one is not proud of that turn out to be humiliating and embarrassing.

Be clever and aware while participating in online social media. Develop smart online practices and learn what is appropriate to share, how to share it and with whom. Some huge sins start out with innocent intentions, just chatting and sharing pictures, which gradually develop into a type of relationship outside of marriage that God forbids. A picture becomes a longer and deeper personal conversation, which becomes a meeting and finally a forbidden romance.

Financial hardship or the emotional need to confide should never be an excuse to let one's guard down, especially for women. When an individual is in a position of financial or emotional need, she is more susceptible to intimidation from men and could be persuaded to do things that she would not consider under normal circumstances. Women, and especially Muslim women, are models of honor and dignity, and do not accept any form of degradation or humiliation. Fear God and remember that He is the ultimate provider and source of comfort.

6. Fulfill Rights and Do Not Shortchange

A righteous man invested the wages for his worker and he gave him the full amount due after it had grown and multiplied. His actions proved that he was both scrupulous and trustworthy. Remember that all of a person's wealth belongs to God, and is given from God as a trust to see how a person will handle the test. When a person thinks only of himself and tries to shortchange others, his wealth will not be blessed and he could lose it all.

7. Sincerity Is the Core of Worship

Be sincere to God in word and action in order to gain His pleasure. God is always watching, ever-present, and He knows one's secrets and the state of one's conscience. As God says in the Quran, "He knows the treachery of the eyes and whatever is concealed by hearts." [8]

---

[8] [Ghafir:19]
All translations of Quranic verses are by Mufti Taqi Usmani (Quran Explorer). "God" has been inserted in place of "Allah" for clarity.

13

It is reported that 'Umar Ibn Al-Khattab (ra) asked 'Ubay Ibn Kaab (ra) about God-consciousness (taqwa). 'Ubay replied, "Have you ever walked through a thorny path?"

'Umar answered, "Yes, indeed."

'Ubay asked him, "What did you do?"

'Umar replied, "I gathered myself together and struggled."

'Ubay said, "That is God-consciousness."

— 3 —

Consciousness of God
The Pious Man and the Apple [9]

Thabit ibn Al-Nu'man, a pious man from among the early Muslims, was very hungry and tired. He passed by an orchard and entered among the trees to rest for a while in the shade. His stomach growled as his gaze rested longingly upon an apple on one of the trees. Out of hunger and sheer fatigue, his hand reached out for the apple. Before he knew it, he had devoured half of the apple before stopping to drink from a nearby creek.

As his hunger subsided, Thabit comprehended the magnitude of his carelessness. Regret set in as he realized that he had neglected to ask the owner's permission to eat the apple. Stricken with remorse, Thabit Ibn Al-Nu'man resolved that he would not leave the orchard until he had found the owner and asked his pardon and forgiveness.

---

[9] Anees Al-Saliheen wa Sameer Al-Muttaqeen, by Muhammad Amin Al-Jundi.

Thabit Ibn Al-Nu'man wandered among the orchard trees until he found the owner's house and knocked on the door. When the owner greeted him, Thabit explained the story of his hunger and the apple, and begged the owner's pardon.

"I entered your orchard next to the creek, and I picked this apple. I ate half of it before realizing that it did not belong to me. I ask that you may pardon me for eating it and forgive me for my mistake," Thabit concluded.

The owner thought for a moment. Then he said, "I will forgive you under one condition."

"What is your condition?" asked Thabit.

"That you marry my daughter," replied the owner.

"I will marry her," Thabit declared.

The owner of the orchard continued, "But you must know that my daughter is blind and cannot see, mute and unable to speak, and deaf, hard of hearing."

Thabit paused as he thought about this dilemma. He wondered how he could take care of such a person and what he should ultimately do. Thabit resolved that taking care of a disabled wife would be better than risking punishment from God for taking property that was not his. Besides, Thabit thought, the days in his lifetime were numbered, compared to the eternity of the afterlife. He took a deep breath and agreed to marry the owner's daughter.

When the wedding day came, Thabit ibn Al-Nu'man was consumed with worry. He wondered if he would be able to communicate with his bride, or if she would even know that he was marrying her. Despite his doubts, he put his trust in God, saying, "There is no power or might other than that of God. We belong to God, and to Him is our final return."

The time came for Thabit to meet his bride. He approached her anxiously. To his surprise, she turned to face him and said brightly, "*Assalamu Alaikum wa Rahmatullahi wa Barakatuhu,*" welcoming him with the customary greeting of peace and blessings. As she spoke, she looked straight into his eyes, her gaze firmly fixed on his own. He looked back at her, awestruck. She was so lovely, he thought, like a heavenly maiden.

After a moment of silence, Thabit finally spoke, "How can this be? You can speak, hear, and see!" He then told his new bride about the description of her that was given to him by her very own father.

"My father told you the truth and was not lying," the young woman stated.

"How so?" asked Thabit.

The bride explained, "He told you I was mute because I do not speak ill of anyone, use bad language, or say anything displeasing to God. I do not carry inappropriate conversations with men. I am deaf because I do not listen to idle conversations or backbiting. Lastly, I am blind because I lower my gaze and do not look at anything forbidden."

It is no wonder that God brought together this righteous man and this God-fearing woman. It is likewise no surprise that from this union came one of the greatest Muslim scholars and jurists, who would fill the world with his knowledge. Their son was none other than Imam Abu Hanifa Al-Nu'man.

Lessons Learned:

1. **Holding Oneself to Account Is a Quality of the God-Fearing**

   Holding oneself to account every night for the day's actions, as God has advised, purifies the deeds and warrants forgiveness for mistakes that were made throughout the day. Admonishing oneself also opens the door to repentance, and to seeking the forgiveness of others who may have been wronged. Without reviewing one's deeds, mistakes are overlooked and sins can take over the heart. Feeling remorse is the key to sincerely seeking forgiveness before it is too late.

2. **Seeking Permission Is a Sign of Piety**

   Many have gotten into the habit of taking food or minor supplies from school, work, or the mosque without asking permission first, either because one does not know to whom they may belong, or one assumes that no one will mind. Even if this is sometimes the case, at other times the owner might consider the food or goods to have been stolen. Never take anything before seeking permission in order to avoid consuming the unlawful, God forbid.

3. **Being Punished in Life Is Better than in the Hereafter**

   This pious man compared the trouble he would be facing during his life to the eternal punishment of the Hereafter. Only then could he accept his worldly fate. All believers should realize that no matter how severe a sin's punishment might be, it will still be short and fleeting compared to what the alternative is in the Hereafter. If people admit mistakes, seek forgiveness, and repent immediately, they will find God helping them and easing their way.

4. **Whoever Fears God, He Brings Forth a Way Out for Him, and Provides Him from Where He Does Not Even Imagine** [10]

Thabit was patient with the hardship he faced. He sought God's assistance by saying, "We belong to God, and to Him is our final return." As a result, God relieved his hardship and replaced it with the comfort of having a blessed, pious, healthy wife. He was further blessed with a righteous son who filled the world with his knowledge and whose books are still studied today. For raising such a pious son, Thabit Bin Al-Nu'man and his wife shared in the reward of their son's lofty accomplishments. Every believer must ask himself or herself, have I truly feared God so that I may receive such rewards?

5. **Deaf, Mute, and Blind: Attributes of a Believer**

What comes to mind when mentioning these attributes is that they are qualities of deficiency and disability. In reality, a believer might only wish to be blind from seeing improper sights. It is difficult to avoid seeing inappropriate public displays, partly due to the widespread exposure in current times and modern technology. Similarly, it would be a blessing to be deaf from listening to indecent music, pointless gossip, or callous back-biting. Finally, to be mute from speaking insults, lies, or harsh jokes would only be for the better.

6. **To One Who Acts for the Sake of God, God Brings Worldly and Eternal Success**

Thabit Bin Al-Nu'man accepted to marry a young woman with many deficiencies just to fix an

---

[10] [Al-Talaq:2-3]

unintentional mistake. He was willing to pay this high price because pleasing God was more valuable to him than anything else in the world. For this reason, God rewarded Thabit with a pious wife who was in reality a good match for him. God blessed the marriage, and the resulting offspring. Whatever begins in goodness concludes in goodness.

7. Welcome Suitors Who Are God-Fearing

The father chose to offer his daughter in marriage to a passerby because of the stranger's righteousness. He was sure that this God-fearing young man would take good care of her, fear God in fulfilling her rights, and treat her well and fairly. Choose good character as the most important factor in a suitor, over outward appearances, notable lineage, education, or wealth. In doing so, parents fulfill what God has entrusted upon them: to marry their son or daughter to a suitable mate. By doing so, they have also entrusted their child to someone capable of treating him or her with the best of care.

"Whoever is preoccupied by the material world, God will hinder his affairs and keep him in constant fear of poverty. He will not get anything more from the world except that which was allotted to him. Whoever makes the Hereafter his preoccupation, God will settle his affairs for him, place freedom from want in his heart, and his provisions and worldly gain will undoubtedly come to him."

Prophet Muhammad (PBUH)
Narrated by Ahmed, Ibn Majah, and Tirmidhi

— 4 —

God Is the Provider

The Daughter of Hatim Al-Asam [11]

There once lived a man named Hatim Al-Asam, who lived with his family in their small home. He was a poor man who barely had enough money to feed his family. But Hatim had set his intention to make pilgrimage (*Hajj*), even though he scarcely had the means to do so. So one evening, Hatim gathered his family to tell them that he intended to make pilgrimage to Mecca. Surprised by the father's decision, nearly everyone in the household was troubled and concerned. They cried out to their father, "Under whose care will you be leaving us? We are so poor. We have no one but you!"

The entire family argued and voiced their disapproval, except for Hatim's youngest daughter. As the family members tried to convince the father to abandon his plan, she turned

---

[11] Dalil Al-Sa'ileen, pg. 139, by Anas Ismail Abu Dawud.

to the rest of the family and spoke up. "Listen everyone! Please let him be! He is not the one who provides for us. God is our true provider, and God will continue to provide for us in our father's absence!" she exclaimed.

The young girl's convincing words and strong conviction had a clear effect on the family. They dismissed their concerns and gave him their blessings to set out upon the sacred journey. Hatim Al-Asam packed his meager belongings and began his travel.

After a few days, the family began to feel the absence of their father. They began to go to sleep hungry, without food to quiet their growling stomachs. As time went by, the other children blamed their sister for convincing them to allow their father to leave. Distraught and lonely, the young girl turned to God in supplication, asking Him not to leave her humiliated and disgraced in front of her family. The days grew longer, the entire family grew hungrier, and the blame upon the little girl grew more intense.

On one of these hungry nights, the ruler of the kingdom was returning from a hunting trip with his soldiers. As they passed through the town on their journey home, the ruler was quite thirsty. He asked for his vessel of water, but he opened it only to discover that it was empty. They searched for another vessel, but there was no water left among the entire troop. The thirsty ruler ordered his soldiers to stop by the nearest home to ask for water.

The first home they came to was none other than that of Hatim Al-Asam's family. The soldiers knocked on the door and requested some water for the thirsty ruler. Hatim's family graciously obliged, providing the soldiers with jugs of water to take back with them. At long last, the cool water ran down the leader's parched throat. With great relief, his thirst was quenched and strength regained.

"How refreshing this water was! Who provided it for us?" asked the ruler.

The soldiers informed the ruler that it was the home of Hatim Al-Asam, a man known in the kingdom for being kind-hearted and honest. But Hatim was not home, the soldiers explained, for he had left to make pilgrimage and his poor, hungry family was on its own.

When he heard this, the ruler swiftly removed the exquisite gold belt he was wearing and cast it aside. He told his companions, "If I am beloved to you, then you should do the same." Soon everyone began removing their valuables, and the pile of riches grew larger and larger. The soldiers visited the home once again, but this time they presented the mound of wealth as a gift to the family of Hatim Al-Asam.

The family was overjoyed. They could hardly believe that in a matter of minutes, they had gone from having nothing to eat to owning great riches. They were struck with awe by the generosity of the ruler and his men. The family celebrated and rejoiced in their good fortune, except for the little girl, who sat alone in the corner. Her cheeks were wet from her tears.

"Why are you crying? Praise be to God, who has bestowed great blessings upon us!" her mother said, trying to comfort her.

The girl looked up at her mother with her tearful eyes and said, "One of God's creations took one glance at us and brought us all of these blessings. What must happen, then, when the Creator looks upon us?"

24

Lessons Learned:

1. Do Not Jump to Conclusions

The family was reluctant to allow Hatim Al-Asam to perform the pilgrimage because they depended on him to provide for them. Once he left, they were afraid that they would have almost nothing to eat for months until his return. The family judged their situation superficially by how their circumstances outwardly appeared. Yet once the father left, they were provided for in a way that they could never have imagined. What's more, Hatim was also provided with the reward of making pilgrimage. Do not judge situations by their outward appearances, and leave matters up to God.

2. God Is the Provider

Most do not have the true conviction that God is the ultimate provider, but the little girl had great understanding of this meaning. She knew that her father tried his best to provide for the family, but God was their true provider in the end. Even if the father left and the food diminished, their true provider was still with them. Never fear loss of provision, for God never forgets anyone.

3. Be Patient and Avoid Rushing

Although the family was at first convinced that God would provide for them in the father's absence, the delay in provision brought them to question, ridicule, and taunt the young girl who had persuaded them. They quickly grew impatient, as if they doubted God's decree. It is not uncommon for people to fall into this same trap. Despite knowing and believing that God is the provider, many feel anxious when their provision does not come immediately. This type of impatience is rooted in a weakness of faith, and God knows best.

4. Taking the Proper Means When Faced with Hardships

As the family grew more and more restless to receive their provision, the wise young girl was certain that God would soon bless them. To seek out their provision, the girl took the proper means. She prayed to God, doing her part, while still relying entirely upon God. She also asked God not to allow her to remain humiliated in front of her family. As a result, God eased things for the family and granted them much more than they could have imagined.

5. The Ruler Sets the Example in Thanking People

The ruler did not take any more than a vessel of water from the home of Hatim Al-Asam. Yet he still wanted to thank them for it, especially after he found out that the father was a good man away on pilgrimage. He sought to reward the righteous and tend to the needs of those less fortunate. The ruler also wanted to spread the reward from God for his good deed, so he invited his soldiers to participate in the opportunity as well. One should not forget to thank those who do even the smallest good deed, and to encourage others to participate in good acts so that they may also receive the reward.

6. The Generosity of Man Cannot Compare to the Generosity of the Creator

Reflect upon God's incredible generosity toward His creation. God simply brought the ruler to be touched by the family's kind deed, and it ended in tremendous prosperity for the family. Be thankful to God and ask from God. God's incredible generosity will surely follow. Realize that God's generosity is not limited to material things. He may also bless one with inner wealth, such as the blessing of true faith or good health. He may even conceal one's mistakes, or make people beloved to one another. These are just a few of the countless number of blessings from God that are often taken for granted until they have been lost.

"We will show them Our signs in the universe and within their own beings until it will become manifest to them that it is the truth. Is it not enough about your Lord that He is witness to everything?"

[Fussilat:53]

— 5 —
God Is Ever-Witnessing
The Log [12]

A man from among the Children of Israel asked another to lend him one thousand dinars.

He answered, "Bring me a witness to observe the transaction."

The man replied, "God is sufficient as the witness."

So he said, "Then bring a guarantor."

---

[12] Hadith of the Prophet Muhammad (pbuh), related by Abu Hurairah, narrated by Bukhari.

"God is adequate as the guarantor," the man declared.

He said, "You have spoken the truth." So he lent the man one thousand dinars, to be returned at an agreed-upon time.

Soon after, the man who borrowed the money went out to sea to complete his business. After taking care of his affairs, the man searched for a boat in order to return so that he could repay his debt on time. But the man simply could not find a boat that could take him back.

Instead, he found a log. So the man took the log and carved a hole in it. He then stuffed the log with one thousand dinars, as well as a letter addressing its rightful owner. The man plugged and sealed the hole, then he took the stuffed piece of wood with him to the seashore.

Once he arrived at the shore, the man proclaimed, "Dear God, You surely know that I borrowed one thousand dinars from So-and-so. He had asked me for a guarantor, and I said 'God is adequate as the guarantor,' and he agreed to that. He also asked me to bring a witness, and I replied, 'God is sufficient as a witness,' and that was enough for him. I have searched for a boat to return what belongs to him, and I have not been able to find one. So now I entrust you with it." With that, the man threw the log into the sea. The man left, but continued to search for a boat to take him back to his debtor all the while.

Some time later, the man's lender went out to the shore to see if perhaps a ship had arrived with his money, but instead all he found was a log washed upon the shore. He decided to take the log home as firewood for his family. But as he began to chop it, he found the money inside, as well as the letter.

Days later, the man who borrowed the money found a

boat to take him back and finally arrived. He had brought with him an additional one thousand dinars and presented it to his lender, apologizing for the delay. He explained, "By God, I struggled to find a boat to return me here, and I only just found the one I have come by."

The lender asked, "Did you send something out to me?"

The man repeated, "I could not find a boat before the one upon which I just came.'"

He said, "God has indeed delivered on your behalf what you sent out in the log, so you may keep your one thousand dinars. May you continue to remain guided on the right path."

Lessons Learned:

1. God Helps Those Who Help God's Servants

This lender was quick to help another in his hardship, and this was his only concern. He was also satisfied with God as the witness and the guarantor on the loan. The lender understood that once he helped the man, God would surely help him. The Prophet (pbuh) taught this as he said, "Whoever removes a trouble for a fellow believer in this world, God will remove one of his troubles on the Day of Judgment. And whoever eases things for another in hardship, God will ease things for him in this world and the Hereafter. And whoever conceals the faults and sins of a Muslim, God will conceal his faults and sins in this world and in the Hereafter. God helps His servant as long as His servant helps his brother." [13] Always seek to help people and ease their troubles. Do not seek out their gratitude or praise in return, because God's assistance and reward is much greater.

2. God Is Sufficient as a Witness and a Guarantor

In every transaction, it is critical to protect the rights of all parties by taking all practical means, including the presence of witnesses and guarantors. This prevents a person from falling victim to temptations, forgetting, taking advantage of others, lying, or cheating. While some cheat the system, break the law, and abuse their authority, others turn a blind eye to these wrongs. Remember that God's gaze is never averted. He witnesses everything, and He is angered by such actions.

---

[13] Narrated by Muslim.

3. Believers Keep Their Promises

The man was eager to return the borrowed funds to his lender within the time frame that he promised. When he could not find a boat, he sent it in a log, hoping it would arrive at the right place and on time. Yet he did not just depend on the log and leave the matter at that. He had a second set of funds prepared, and he continued his quest to find a boat so that he might return the money to the man with his own two hands. When he finally found a boat, he returned the money and apologized for the delay. Adhering to appointments and arriving at an agreed-upon time are from good character, and so is fulfilling trusts. Offering apologies or excuses as to why there was not enough time or money to keep one's promise has unfortunately become the norm. The Prophet (pbuh) spoke of this when he said, "The signs of a hypocrite are three: when he speaks, he lies; when he promises, he breaks it; and when he is given a trust, he betrays it." [14]

4. Supplication and Entrusting God

The borrower took all possible means to return the money to its owner. He took physical means by sending money with a letter in the log. But he also took spiritual means, by entrusting God and praying to Him that the money would return to its rightful owner. Finally, he took practical means, by continuing his search for a boat so that he might return the funds in person. The man had a good opinion of God and entrusted Him with the safe return of the money. And indeed, the money did arrive to its owner on time.

---

[14] Bukhari and Muslim.

33

5. Honesty and Trustworthiness Are Qualities of the Righteous

The lender was honest with the borrower by letting him know that he had found the money in the log. He could have easily hidden the fact that he had already received the money in order to keep the second sum for himself as well. Instead, he did not hesitate to share the news that he already received his full due. His actions teach a powerful lesson of honesty, trustworthiness, personal accountability, and God-consciousness. How many today would really do the same, to be satisfied with receiving what one was actually due, instead of greedily accepting what someone, an individual or business, may unknowingly overpay?

"Oh, Child of Adam, between you and God you have committed many mistakes and sins that no one knows of except for Him, and you would love that God forgive you for them. So if you desire God's forgiveness for them, then you should be forgiving to His servants. And if you would love His pardon, then you should pardon His servants. For truly the reward comes in the same form as the deed."

Ibn Qayyim Al-Jawziyya

— 6 —

Belief in Judgment Day
The Man from Paradise [15]

One day, we were sitting with the Prophet (pbuh) when he said, "A man from Paradise will now appear before us." Soon after, a man from the citizens of Medina (*Ansar*) approached, his beard dripping with water from ablution (*wudu*), clutching both of his sandals in his left hand.

The next day, the Prophet (pbuh) made the statement again, and the very same man came as he did the day before. On the third day, the Prophet spoke of the same thing once again. For a third time, the man approached in the same manner as he had done the first time.

---

[15] Hadith of the Prophet Muhammad (pbuh), related by Anas Ibn Malik, narrated by Imam Ahmed Ibn Hanbal in his book Al-Musnad, as written in the book Al-Anqiyaa', pg. 22-23, by Ibrahim ibn Abdullah Al-Duwaish.

After the Prophet (pbuh) left, Abdullah ibn 'Amr (ra) [16] decided to follow the man. He approached the man and said, "My father and I have quarreled, and I have sworn to stay away from home for three days. I wanted to see if I might stay with you for that time."

"Certainly," the man replied.

Abdullah told us that he stayed with him for three nights. He observed that the man did not get up for worship during the night until the dawn, other than mentioning God when he stirred in his sleep.

Abdullah recalled, "Other than that, I did not hear anything but good from him. So when the three nights were over, I nearly belittled his deeds. I said to him, 'There was no disagreement or bad feelings between me and my father, but I heard the Messenger (pbuh) say, 'A man will now come who is from the people of Paradise,' and you appeared all three times. So I wanted to stay with you to observe your deeds so that I might do the same. I did not see you do extra acts of worship, so what has brought you to attain this status that the Messenger (pbuh) mentioned?'"

The man replied, "I do no more than what you have seen, other than that I do not hold within me resentment toward any Muslim, and I do not envy anyone for the goodness God has given them."

Abdullah said, "Then that is what has brought you to reach this status, and those are the deeds that so few are able to do."

---

[16] Acronym for "radiyya Allahu anhu" which translates to "may God be pleased with him." Common Islamic etiquette encourages such prayers to be made for the companions of the Prophet (pbuh) at the written or spoken mention of their names.

Lessons Learned:

1. **Making Lessons Engaging**

   The Prophet (pbuh) engaged his companions in his unique style of teaching by turning their attention to the man who would be granted Paradise. Because he did not disclose the man's deeds, he made these companions yearn to find the answer and learn the greater lesson on their own. It is crucial to use new methods of teaching in order to uncover deeper truths. Conversely, students must challenge themselves in order to see results. Whatever comes easily without much effort is usually lost easily as well, or taken for granted. And whatever is earned through hard work is usually nurtured, retained, and cherished.

2. **Competing for the Prize: Paradise**

   The Prophet's (pbuh) companion, Abdullah ibn 'Amr, needed to know what deeds had led the man to win the ultimate prize of Paradise. Abdullah certainly wanted to find out in order to imitate the man's actions so that he might earn the same prize. He wasted no time in coming up with a plan in order to place himself in the man's home, without revealing his true intentions. The ambition of the companions in their quest for Paradise was truly unparalleled. Their focus was to compete for rank in the Hereafter. Follow the lead of these righteous believers, and do not make worldly gain life's main competition.

3. **Status Cannot Be Judged by Appearance**

   This companion did not appear to be someone of special status in Paradise. He appeared to be very simple by his humble demeanor, as he arrived dripping from his ablution, carrying his sandals in his left hand. Neither was he known among the companions as someone famous for any special actions. Yet God and the Prophet (pbuh) honored him for his heart's good deeds, which would have remained hidden if it was not for the efforts of Abdullah ibn 'Amr. Do not be quick to judge based on outward appearances, but instead look at inward actions.

4. **Watching the Tongue May Lead to Paradise**

This companion had a tongue that mentioned God when he stirred in his sleep, and he did not speak other than good words as Abdullah ibn 'Amr described. The Prophet Muhammad (pbuh) advised one of his companions, Muaz Ibn Jabal (ra), to be careful with his tongue. Muaz had asked him if they would be responsible for what was said by the tongue, to which the Prophet (pbuh) replied, "Will people be thrown face first into the Hellfire because of other than what was earned by their tongues?" [17] Deeds are judged by the words of the tongue as well as the intention of the heart. The tongue was the first reason that this companion earned Paradise. Be among those who watch their words carefully. By doing so, it is possible to be beloved by people in this world, and rewarded by God in the next.

5. **Believing in Accountability and Watching the Heart**

Many do not quickly forgive the hurtful words of others. When a person is hurt by words, it has unfortunately become common practice to reply with words that are ten times harsher. Often, the purpose of this defensive response is to show no sign of weakness. Thus, people take it upon themselves to speak out in retaliation. It is often forgotten that God

---
[17] Tirmidhi.

is watching, and He rewards each action as it deserves. Do not take these measures, but rather, remember the actions of this wise companion. Have faith in God's accountability. Go to sleep with no resentment, envy, or enmity toward anyone. Forgive others often. Those who do so will find God pardoning their own sins, and they will be granted the greatest reward of Paradise.

6. Revealing the Truth

The story raises an obvious question: how could the companion Abdullah ibn 'Amr tell a lie in order to find out the information he sought? When he shared his story about his father with the man, his intention was to uncover the good deeds and reveal the secret behind the man's tremendous reward. He wanted to share the goodness with the other believers and, because of his effort, the man's actions are still shared with people today. Additionally, Abdullah ibn 'Amr did reveal the truth to the man as soon as he finished observing him, so that he would not deceive him.

"Whoever gives in charity, even the value of a date, from pure earnings, and God does not accept other than what is pure, it is as if he placed it in the right palm of God to raise it for him just as one of you raises a mare, until it is like a mountain."

Prophet Muhammad (PBUH)
Related by Abu Hurairah, Narrated by Bukhari and Muslim

— 7 —

Prosperous Charity
Imam Ali and Fatima Al-Zahra [18]

A poor man came to the door of Ali ibn Abi Talib (ra) one day. When he saw the needy man, Ali said to his son Hasan (ra), "Go to your mother and tell her of the six dirhams I had given her, to give me one dirham."

Hasan did as he was told, went to his mother, and requested the money. He returned to his father and said, "She said that you gave her the six dirhams to buy flour."

Ali thought for a moment. He said, "The faith of a servant is not sincere until he values what is in God's hands more than he values what is in his very own hands. Tell her, my son, to give me all six dirhams."

Hasan went back to his mother, and he returned to his father with the six dirhams. Without hesitating, Ali gave the

---

[18] Dalil Al-Sa'ileen, pg. 398, by Anas Ismail Abu Dawud.

entire amount to the needy man.

Only a short time had passed when Ali noticed a man along the way who had a fine camel for sale. Ali asked the man, "How much is your camel for sale, oh, Sir?"

The man replied, "It is for sale for one hundred and forty dirhams."

Ali said, "You can sell it to me, but I hope that you would be willing to postpone its payment for eight days." The man agreed. Ali took the camel and tied it in front of his home.

A short time later, another man was passing by Ali's home. He asked, "To whom does this camel belong?" looking at the camel that Ali had just purchased.

Ali replied, "This is my camel."

"Would you be willing to sell it?" the man asked.

"Certainly," Ali said.

"For how much?" the man asked.

"Two hundred dirhams," Ali replied.

"Agreed," the man said. He took the camel and paid Ali the full payment of two hundred dirhams.

Ali went back to the man whom he owed payment for the camel, and he gave him the promised one hundred and forty dirhams.

Ali then took the remaining sixty dirhams home to his wife Fatima.

"What is this?" Fatima asked, as Ali presented the money to her.

Ali replied, "This is what God has promised, when He said, 'Whoever comes with a good deed will receive ten times as much, and whoever comes with an evil deed will be requited with no more than the like of it, and they shall not be wronged.'" [19]

[19] [Al-Anaam:160]

Lessons Learned:

1. Never Denying Those in Need

The companions of the Prophet (pbuh) were careful to remember the poor and needy and to care for them. They did not deny them charity, belittle them, or look down upon them. They sympathized with their needs, and they understood the tremendous reward that awaited them for helping the poor, as promised by God. God mentions in the Quran, "And as for the beggar, do not scold him." [20]

Unfortunately, today some people may pretend to be needy in order to cheat others out of money. They wrongfully use this money to build mansions or to do unlawful things. However, these beggars should not be a discouragement from giving generously to the needy. When in doubt, give food or clothing instead of giving money so that it is not misspent improperly or extravagantly.

2. A Test of One's Faith

When Imam Ali sent his son to his wife to fetch money for the needy man, Fatima sent back the message that the money was set aside for flour. But Ali wanted to prove to the family that what God had in store for them would be greater than what they had in their hands. For this reason, he gave the needy man all of the money they had. Ali set an example that faith should not be hollow, but must be reinforced with actions. Faith is like a tree, and actions are the core. Without the core, a tree is hollow and weak, and may fall over from the lightest breeze.

---

[20] [Ad-Dhuha:10]

3. The Blessings of Trade

Many people prefer to be an employee because of its benefits, such as job security, stability, and a guaranteed paycheck of a set amount. They do not want to deal with risk and fluctuation with regards to profit or loss. But earning a living through trade is a blessing, and it can be very profitable as well. God mentions in the Quran, "And others traveling in the land, seeking the grace of God." [21] Trade also teaches one to rely upon and trust entirely in God. As the Prophet (pbuh) said, "If you were to rely upon God as He deserves to be relied upon, He would provide for you as He provides for the birds. They go out early in the morning hungry and return in the evening full." [22] It is very beneficial to engage in trade, even in simple ways or on a small scale, in order to receive the blessings of trade and potentially large profits, as was the case for Ali ibn Abi Talib.

4. Charity Multiplies

God has promised that giving charity will never decrease one's wealth. Rather, it will do the opposite. The Prophet (pbuh) said, "Charity does not decrease wealth. No servant forgives except that God increases his honor, and no one humbles himself for the sake of God except that God raises his status." [23] Indeed, God will multiply the wealth of one who gives charity, as God says, "Whoever does a good deed, God will reward it ten times its amount." Give generously, and do not fear loss or poverty. Rest assured that whatever is given away, God will return manifold.

---

[21] [Al-Muzzammil:20]
[22] Narrated by Tirmidhi and Ahmed.
[23] Narrated by Muslim.

5. Charity from Primary Wealth, Not Just from Excess Wealth

Many who give charity only give from their extra wealth. Often they live extravagantly in large mansions and drive luxury cars, spend generously on themselves and their children, eat only the best food, and wear only the finest clothing. It is often forgotten that charity is supposed to be given from one's main wealth, and not just from one's excess. Charity blesses a person's primary wealth from which it was paid. Donating also protects the one who gives it, eases one's hardships, heals the ill in the household, and wards off difficult circumstances. Be like the companions and the righteous who gave out charity in place of spending on their main necessities. They did not deny those who were needy, for they even gave away money set aside for main staples, such as flour for making bread to feed their own children.

6. Selling on Credit

Imam Ali bought the camel and took it home, but he delayed the payment for eight days. This shows that it is indeed allowed to buy and sell on credit. Both sides must agree to the terms, neither side may be cheated, and the agreement should not approach what God has deemed unlawful. This also illustrates that Islam makes things easy and encourages buying and selling transactions in trade, and God knows best.

A person's life will one day turn into a book. Make the topics beautiful, for one day every individual will be reading his or her own chapters. God says, "Read your book. Enough are you today to take your own account."

[Al-Isra:14]

— 8 —

The Charity of Words
The Persian King and the Old Farmer [24]

A long time ago, there was a Persian king named Anusharwan, during whose reign the Prophet Muhammad (pbuh) was born. One day, the king announced throughout his kingdom that whomever said a good word would be awarded four hundred dinars.

Days later, the king was walking with his entourage in the city when he saw an elderly farmer in his nineties. He observed the old man planting an olive tree, as he watered and tended to the young sapling.

"Why are you caring for this young olive tree that will need twenty years before it will bear fruit, while you are an elderly man in your nineties whose days are surely numbered?" the king asked.

---

[24] Magazine article, Qissat Al-Islam, by L.B. Arsalan.

The old farmer said, "Those before us planted, and we enjoyed their harvest. So we plant for those who come after us to benefit from the harvest."

"Well said," the king remarked. "Those were indeed good words that you have spoken." So the king ordered that the farmer be given four hundred dinars.

The old man took the gracious gift and smiled widely. The king asked, "Why are you smiling?"

"The tree will not bear olives for twenty years, but my tree did bear its fruit now," replied the old man.

"Very nice, indeed. Give him another four hundred dinars," the king ordered.

The farmer accepted the gift and smiled once again. "Why do you smile now?" asked the king.

"The olive tree will only bring fruit once a year, but my tree has already brought me fruit twice," the farmer said, as he continued to grin widely.

"Well spoken. Give him four hundred dinars once more," commanded the king. And with that, the king left quickly.

"Why did you hasten to leave so quickly?" the king's chief officer asked.

The king replied, "If I remained there until the morning, the treasury would be empty while the good words of the old farmer would not have ended."

Lessons Learned:

1. Taking a Walk

All types of people, from kings to scholars, can benefit from taking an occasional walk. Whether it is for recreation or to clear one's mind, taking a walk makes the body active. The change of environment can energize, refresh, and take one out of a rut from a stale environment or a boring work routine. Taking a walk calms the nerves, relieves mental tension, boosts energy, and refreshes the mind to reflect about God's creation.

2. The Wisdom of the King

The king wanted to encourage the use of kind words throughout the kingdom. He understood that if people spoke good words, it would play a part in improving society. Many crimes begin from interpersonal conflicts that are triggered by bad words. Envy, hatred, gossip, lies, and insults all play a role in escalating a conflict into a major crime, such as theft, slander, and murder. The king understood that if he encouraged the citizens to speak good words, there would be greater morality in their society and the entire kingdom would be better. Spread good words for the betterment of the community as well as for self-improvement.

3. Saying Kind Words Is Charity

Out of the king's wisdom, he urged his people to use good language, and he motivated them by offering the reward of four hundred dinars. When the religion of Islam came, it reinforced the merits of saying good words and encouraged these verbal actions by deeming them a form of charity. The reward for a kind word is equal to donating money in charity. The Prophet (pbuh) said, "Charity is due for every joint in your body, on every day the sun comes up. To act justly between two people is a charity. To help a man with his mount, lifting him onto it, or hoisting his belongings onto it, is charity. A good word is charity. Every step taken towards prayer is charity, and removing a harmful thing from the road is charity." [25] So, say good words, and receive the reward from God that has no end.

4. The Wisdom of "They Planted and We Harvested"

The farmer showed his profound wisdom in his statement explaining why such an elderly man should continue to plant a tree from which he will never eat. Every person should remain active and productive until the very last moment of life. The Prophet (pbuh) encouraged this by saying, "If the last hour comes and in your hand there is a seedling, then plant it you are able to do so." [26] Be among those who continue to work in order to benefit all of those who are around. Make it a personal goal to help build the community and the nation, not just the individual.

5. Good Deeds Bring Blessings to the Righteous

Notice that the good words of the farmer were rewarded quickly. This will often happen, as God said, "If the people of the towns believed and feared God, We would have opened for them blessings from the heavens and the earth." [27] This farmer was righteous in the words he spoke, so God blessed and provided for him, and allowed his "tree" to bring him immediate fruit. When people work hard and speak only good, they will find God providing His bounty and blessings

---

[25] Narrated by Bukhari and Muslim.
[26] Narrated by Ahmed.
[27] [Al-Araf:96]

in all of their actions.

6. Wisdom Is the Lost Property of the Believer, Take It from Wherever It Is Found

The king was willing to take wisdom from the elderly farmer, so much so that he was worried his treasury would go bankrupt from rewarding the farmer for all of the wisdom he might share. Do not be too proud to learn a lesson from someone of lower rank. Instead, keep an open mind and an open heart to take wisdom from wherever it may be found.

"People will be gathered on the Day of Judgment hungrier than they ever were, thirstier than they had ever been, and more bare than ever before. So, whoever fed another for the sake of God will be fed by God. And whoever quenched someone's thirst for the sake of God will be quenched by God. And whoever concealed others for the sake of God will be veiled by God."

Ihya' Ulum Al-Din

— 9 —

Charity and Growing Wealth
The Call from the Clouds [28]

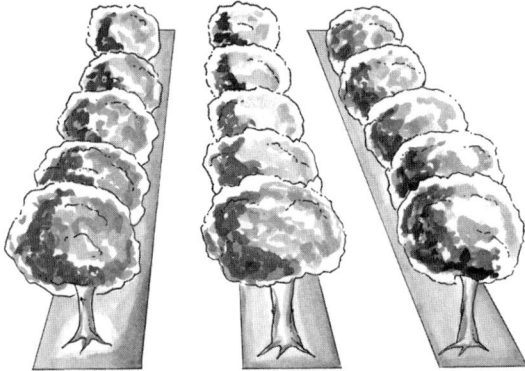

One day a man was passing through a wide, vast dry land. All of a sudden, he heard a voice from the clouds. The voice commanded, "Go and water the land of So-and-so."

The cloud then began moving, until it had floated over an area of rocky land. There it began to pour rain down heavily.

The traveler followed the cloud to the location where it had let down rain. There he found another man. He saw that the man was using a spade to clear a course for the water to stream into his orchard. The man continued to guide the water until he had channeled all of the water to his land.

The curious man went up to the man in the orchard and

---

[28] Hadith of the Prophet Muhammad (pbuh), related by Abu Hurairah, narrated by Muslim.

greeted him, "Peace be upon you," and then addressed the man by the same name he had heard from the voice in the clouds.

The man returned the greeting, "And upon you be peace. But how do you know my name?"

"I heard a voice in the clouds that said, 'Water the land of So-and-so,' then the cloud moved over your land and poured down rain. So what is it that you do exactly?" the man asked.

The owner of the orchard replied, "Since you have asked, I wait until I have harvested all of the produce from my land to then divide it into three parts. One portion I give to charity, one portion I keep to consume for myself and my family, and one portion I reinvest into my orchard."

Lessons Learned:

1. Giving Charity Protects Wealth

The Prophet (pbuh) taught that God will protect one's wealth when a portion of it is given in charity. The Prophet (pbuh) said, "Protect your property with charity (*zakah*), treat illness with charity (*sadaqah*), and face the waves of tribulation with supplication (*duaa*) and humility." [29] Be from among those who fulfill God's rights in one's wealth, and do not be stingy, lest all of the wealth and its blessings be depleted. Remember that a person's wealth actually belongs to God, and that He has simply entrusted individuals with it. Therefore, return it to God in the best of ways that are pleasing to Him.

2. The Reward of Spending on One's Family

The story illustrates the importance of spending on one's own family. Spending on one's family for necessities, such as food, as well as nonessentials, such as gifts and trips, is both praiseworthy and commendable. The Prophet (pbuh) said, "It is sin enough for a man to neglect someone whom he is supposed to feed." [30] It is out of God's wisdom that He requires the head of the household to spend on his children, wife, and parents. Spending on his family is not considered charity because it is an obligation for him to take care of them, yet he is still rewarded.

3. Practical Means and Reinvestment

The story teaches that one must always take the necessary, practical means in order to get results. The man invested a portion of his wealth with God by giving charity, but he also reinvested a portion

---

[29] Narrated by Al-Bayhaqi.
[30] Narrated by Ahmed and Abu Dawud.

of his wealth into his land. This balanced, practical approach ensured that he would continue to grow bountiful crops and maintain good production year after year. In doing so, he also earned a reward. As the Prophet (pbuh) said, "A servant does not plant a crop or sow a seed from which a person, animal, or bird eats except that he will be rewarded." [31] Learn from this man; neither spend all of what one has earned, nor give everything in one's possession to charity, but rather remember to leave a portion for the family, and a portion to invest.

4. God Has Angels Protect the Deeds of the Righteous

The man in the story fulfilled God's right by giving charity and providing for the poor from what God provided him. He also fulfilled the rights of his family, including his own, by spending on his household. Lastly, he fulfilled the rights of the community by maintaining and improving his land and property. God commanded the angels in turn to circle the man's land, bless his orchard with water from the clouds, and protect his earnings and his wealth. This was certainly because he took on the responsibility to fulfill all of these rights. God does not forget one who fulfills obligations to Him, to family, and to the community.

5. Storytelling as a Method of Teaching

The Prophet (pbuh) wanted to teach his companions three valuable lessons. He used this story to convey the lessons quickly and effectively. Be creative and innovative in teaching methods so that lessons are easy to grasp. Use a variety of methods, and remember the impact of a story.

---

[31] Narrated by Bukhari.

"Among what reached the people from the words of earlier prophethood: If you feel no shame, then do whatever you wish."

Prophet Muhammad (PBUH)
Narrated by Bukhari

— 10 —
Shame Before God
Imam Ahmed and His Neighbor [32]

One of the neighbors of Imam Ahmed ibn Hanbal was known among the people for his rebellious actions and disobedience to God. But one day, this neighbor came to the gathering of Imam Ahmed and greeted him.

Imam Ahmed returned the greeting, but the neighbor felt that he had been slighted. The Imam had overlooked him, he thought, and he did not pay him any attention. The neighbor asked the Imam, "Why have you ignored me? I had a vivid dream, and because of it I have changed my ways from how you knew me."

"And what did you see in your dream?" Imam Ahmed asked, now turning his full attention to the man.

---

[32] Story related by Jafar Al-Saigh in Kitab al-Tawwabeen, by Ibn Qudamah Al-Maqdisi.

"In my dream, I saw the Prophet (pbuh) in an area raised above the ground, and many people were sitting below. One person after the next approached him and asked the Prophet (pbuh) to supplicate to God on his behalf. They continued to do so until no one was left except for me. I wanted to also approach him, but I hesitated. I was so ashamed of the horrible sins I was committing.

"Instead, he asked me, 'Oh So-and-so, why do you not come and ask me to supplicate for you?'

"I replied, 'Oh Messenger of God, I only avoid you out of embarrassment from the foul nature of my deeds.'

"He said, 'If it is your shame that holds you back, then stand and ask me to supplicate for you, for you were never one to speak ill of my companions.' So I stood before him and he supplicated for me. And I have since changed my bad actions, for God made sinning detestable to me."

Imam Ahmed turned to the others and said, "Oh, Jafar, oh, Such-and-such, relate this to others, and remember it well, for this is truly beneficial."

Lessons Learned:

1. Condemning the Forbidden, Even Just Within the Heart

Imam Ahmed knew that his neighbor openly committed sins, so he did not greet him with much enthusiasm. Yet he avoided exposing his neighbor's shortcomings to everyone in the gathering, even after the man confronted him for ignoring him. Imam Ahmed acknowledged his neighbor in a way that was meant for only the man to understand, and not the others around them. In this way, he was able to express his disapproval without revealing the man's faults. The Prophet (pbuh) said, "Whoever amongst you sees an evil must then change it with his hand. If he is not able to do so, then with his tongue. If he is not even able to do so, then with his heart, and that is the weakest of faith." [33] Use wisdom when dealing with those who persist in their sins. Be careful not to show acceptance of their behavior, and also not to allow their behavior to affect one's own.

2. Disobedience Is Humiliating

Imam Ahmed's neighbor was humiliated by his sins. His disobedience made others lose respect for him. Once he repented and changed his ways, he had to make it known publicly in order to begin earning back the respect of others. Just as God has mentioned, "As for those who commit evils, the recompense of each evil shall be similar to that evil, and disgrace shall cover them. For them, there is none to save from God. Their faces will seem to be covered with layers of a dark night. Those are the people of the Fire. Therein they shall live forever." [34] Should anyone really accept

---

[33] Narrated by Muslim.
[34] [Yunus:27]

for oneself such humiliation, loss of honor, and lack of dignity? Repent from sins to illuminate the heart and face with the light of obedience to God. Be of those whom God has elevated in status in this world through obedience, and in the Afterlife will gain Paradise.

3. Dreams Can Have Dramatic Impact

Perhaps this man did a good deed, after all, that brought him to see the Prophet (pbuh) in his dream. This dream had a lasting impact, for it finally gave him the motivation he needed to repent and change for the better. It was also a huge honor, because whoever sees the Prophet (pbuh) in a dream has actually seen him. The Prophet (pbuh) mentioned this: "He who has seen me in a dream has certainly seen me, for the Devil cannot take my form." [35]

4. Shame Before God

Many people disobey God, but they fear people finding out about it. They would be ashamed if their family or friends knew of their sins. Yet they feel no shame in front of God, who has given them all of their countless blessings. The Prophet (pbuh) taught the companions how to feel shame before God. He told them, "'Be shy before God most high, as is His due.' We (the companions) said, 'All praise be to God: we are shy of Him.' The Messenger (pbuh) said, 'That is not what is meant. Whoever is shy before God to the extent that is His due should protect his head and that which it includes (i.e., mind, mouth, ears, etc.), his stomach and that which it contains (i.e., preserve it from consuming unlawful food), and he should remember death, and that which is to come after it, and whoever seeks the Hereafter should abandon the adornments of this world. Whoever fulfills these

---

[35] Narrated by Muslim.

duties has been shy before God to the extent that is His full due." [36]

5. Supplication, a Tool to Purify the Heart

The man's dream showed people asking the Prophet (pbuh) to supplicate for them. His supplication helped purify their hearts and change their bad habits. The Prophet taught that supplication is a tool to purify the heart from disobedience. Always begin by asking for God's help through supplication, for supplication is the heart of worship.

6. Insulting the Companions Is a Sin

The dream emphasized the severity of insulting the Prophet's (pbuh) companions. The Prophet (pbuh) told the man that his sins could be forgiven because he had never insulted the companions. For most sins, one may repent and be forgiven, but defaming the companions is especially grave. Many scholars have differed as to the category to which this sin is classified. Their opinions include that such a sin removes a person from Islam, makes the person a hypocrite, or makes one a sinner. In all cases, it is a very serious offense. The Prophet (pbuh) said, "Love for the Helpers of Medina (*Ansar*) is a sign of faith, and hatred for the Helpers is a sign of hypocrisy." [37]

7. Preserving and Spreading Knowledge

Many people attend lectures and conferences, yet fail to retain or spread the lessons that are learned. For this reason, the early Muslims recorded their knowledge carefully. They knew that it was their responsibility to remember, teach, and spread their knowledge. In this way, Imam Ahmed was following in their footsteps, as he told others to share the lesson. As they passed

---

[36] Narrated by Tirmidhi.
[37] Narrated by Bukhari and Muslim.

on the knowledge, their reward was multiplied. The reward for those who learn and teach others will be like one who struggles for the sake of God. The Prophet (pbuh) said, "Whoever comes to this mosque of mine, and only comes for a good purpose, such as to learn or to teach, his status is like that of one who struggles in the cause of God." [38]

[38] Narrated by Ahmed and Ibn Majah.

"When a person's modesty becomes strengthened, his honor is protected. His faults become buried, and his goodness is widespread. When a person loses his modesty, his happiness goes away. When a person loses his happiness, he is belittled by people and is detested. And whoever is detested is harmed by people. Whoever is harmed feels sadness, and whoever is saddened loses his mind. Whoever loses his mind will have his words held against him rather than in his favor. There is no cure for a person without modesty. There is no modesty for the one who has no loyalty, and there is no loyalty for the one who has no brotherhood. Whoever loses modesty does whatever he wants and says whatever he pleases."

Abu Hatim

— 11 —

The Best to Hire Is the Strong and Trustworthy
Moses and the Daughters at the Well [39]

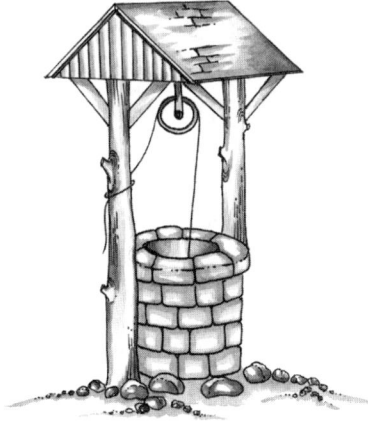

A long time ago, Prophet Moses (as) lived in the land of Egypt. One fateful day, Moses was walking along a path when he saw two men fighting. One of the men was a Jewish man from his people, the Children of Israel. The other was an Egyptian man from the family of Pharaoh.

The man from the Children of Israel called out to Moses to help him in the brawl. Moses swiftly responded to the man's plea and came to break up the fight. Moses pushed the Egyptian man aside. No sooner did Moses shove the man, then the man died right before him. Moses was stricken with remorse for the unintentional killing of this man. He asked for God's forgiveness and declared, "'O my Lord, I have wronged myself, so forgive me.' So He forgave him. Indeed

---

[39] Maa Al-Anbiyaa', pg. 122, by 'Afif Abd Al-Fattah Tabarah

He is the most Forgiving, Very-Merciful." [40]

The next day, the very same Jewish man was yet again in another clash with a new man from the family of Pharaoh. For the second time, the man called out to Moses to come help him. Moses replied to the man, "'You are surely a clear trouble-maker.'" [41]

Still, Moses tried to intervene in order to separate the men and quell the fight. But then the Jewish man drew back and asked Moses, "'Do you want to kill me as you have killed a person yesterday?'" [42] Indeed, he had revealed Moses' mistake by asking the incriminating question.

Moses was worried when he heard the man openly announce the incident from the day before. He let the men be and quickly retreated. But the news that Moses had killed an Egyptian man soon reached Pharaoh and his soldiers. In an effort to protect Moses, one man travelled across the city to warn Moses about the trouble he was about to face from Pharaoh's men. Moses had no choice but to flee Egypt.

As a fugitive on the run, Moses was afraid. He turned to God and supplicated, calling upon Him, "'O my Lord, save me from the cruel people.'" [43] Moses continued moving from place to place until he arrived in the land of Midian, a place that is located in what is now part of southern Palestine.

Once in Midian, Moses stopped to rest near a well. As he sat there, he saw something that disturbed him. He noticed all of the men, who were shepherds drawing water for their livestock, were flocked at the well. The busy men tended to their business, drawing all of the water they needed to give their animals. But there were two women who stood meekly

---

[40] [Al-Qasas:16]
[41] [Al-Qasas:18]
[42] [Al-Qasas:19]
[43] [Al-Qasas:21]

on the side. They waited there patiently, herding their own sheep back from the well. The women were too shy to get the water they needed from the crowded well. The scenario bothered Moses, for he thought it would have been more appropriate for the men to step aside to allow the women to get the water they needed first.

Moses approached the women to ask them about the matter. Just as he had assumed, the women said that they could not get a chance to draw water until the men first took their fill. Furthermore, they explained, their father was quite old and could no longer do this errand for them. So Moses, who was noble and chivalrous, made his way through the crowd of men and graciously fetched the water for the young women.

The women left, and Moses sat under the shade of a tree and prayed to God, "'My Lord, I am in need of whatever good You send down to me.'" [44] Meanwhile, the two young women returned to their father, who was surprised that they were able to return back earlier than usual. He expected them to spend much more time fetching water for the sheep, and he asked them how they had managed to return so promptly. The two girls told their father about the strong, courteous man who drew water on their behalf. He treated them kindly without knowing them or asking for a favor in return. Indeed, he had helped them purely, out of his kindness and decency.

After learning about this, the elderly man asked one of his daughters to go back to Moses and invite him to their home. So the girl returned and bashfully extended the invitation from her father to Moses. She said, "'My father is calling you, so that he may give you a reward for watering our animals.'" [45] Moses accepted the invitation. After Moses arrived and met the old man, Moses shared his story. The

---

[44] [Al-Qasas:24]
[45] [Al-Qasas:25]

father reassured Moses and said, "'Do not fear; you have escaped from the wrongdoing people.'" [46]

One of the girls, out of her wisdom, good judgment, and foresight, suggested to her father what would be truly in the best interest of both Moses and the elderly man. "One of the two women said, 'Dear father, hire him; the best man you can hire is someone who is strong, trustworthy.'" [47] Her father was convinced by her wise suggestion, for Moses would be a very suitable hire.

The father, who was none other than Prophet Shuaib (as) [48], was impressed by Moses' character, work ethic, and demeanor. He offered Moses to marry one of his daughters in exchange for eight years of labor, or up to ten years if Moses was willing to complete them. Moses agreed. He married one of the daughters and worked for Shuaib for the full duration of ten years. Moses remained under the protection of the noble family, and he lived happily with his wife in the land of Midian.

---

[46] [Al-Qasas:25]

[47] [Al-Qasas:26]

[48] Acronym for "alayhi as-salat wa as-salam" which translates to "upon him be prayers and peace." Common Islamic etiquette encourages prayers of peace to be made for the prophets at the written or spoken mention of their names.

Lessons Learned:

1. Decency, Dignity, and Readiness to Help Others Are from Good Character

Out of Moses' decency and dignity, he could not stand by and watch one man take advantage by harming a weaker person. Moses offered his help to end the conflict, but he was lured into a bad situation that led him to push the Egyptian man, who then died. Moses felt bad, blamed himself, and asked for his Lord's forgiveness. He repented wholeheartedly for the unfortunate accident. It is important to be cautious when getting involved in a conflict. It is possible to get caught in the middle and end up being hurt the most by the situation, all for trying to lend a hand. People can end up in a larger dilemma than the one that they are trying to resolve. Be clever in choosing when to get involved, and keep a distance from situations that might backfire.

2. Regret, Repentance, and Asking Forgiveness for Mistakes

When Moses realized that he had killed an innocent man, he repented and asked for God's forgiveness. He recognized that he had wronged another man and declared that he would never do so again, even though the act was unintentional. The fact that it was an accident did not prevent Moses from repenting and blaming himself. People must always take themselves to account and feel remorse for every mistake. After doing something wrong, do not just fault other people or the circumstance. Take responsibility for the mistake, and turn to God in repentance and ask for forgiveness.

3. Do Not Get Burned Twice

Moses saw another fight the following day, and he did not refuse to help when he was asked. But when he saw that it was the same man from the previous day, he recognized that the man was a troublemaker. He left the situation because Moses had no intention to be an aggressor, but rather he was a person whose mission was only to spread peace and righteousness. Avoid falling into someone else's trap. Be wise, and do not make the same mistake twice.

4. Modesty and Keeping a Distance Are Qualities of the Pure

The daughters of Shuaib would rather have kept their distance and returned late than to have asserted themselves among the busy crowd of men. Even when one of them went back to invite Moses, she walked bashfully and approached him shyly. The girls were rewarded, for God provided them with someone to bring them water, and one of them was even given the opportunity to marry a prophet. They were both honored by having their story mentioned by God in the Holy Quran. Remember that modesty is from good character, and God will pair a person of good character with a righteous spouse of equal character. People must be careful not to let their guard down in crowded situations or at mixed gatherings, for modesty must always be carefully guarded.

5. Good Treatment Changes Bad Circumstances

Moses helped the two women in their difficult situation, so God gave him safety and security from his tough circumstance. Moses was also blessed with employment so that he could earn a living, and he was rewarded with a righteous, pure wife. He was even blessed with a place to live, and with a noble family.

All of this was the result of his good treatment toward the women at the well. Be among the people who show only goodness to everyone whose lives they touch, for the reward might even come in this life before the next.

6. A Father's Wisdom and Sensibility

Shuaib was a wise father who noticed the way his daughter was impressed by Moses' character and decency. This was certainly part of the reason that he offered Moses to marry his daughter for ten years of labor in return. Shuaib sets an important example for fathers, to really listen to what their children are saying beyond their words, to understand their feelings and interests. Fathers are tasked not only with understanding what their children are looking for in a spouse, but also making sure suitors are truly suitable in their faith and character. When there is compatibility, it is upon fathers to be reasonable in making the marriage process easy and fair, such as by making the financial expectations smaller or manageable, just as Shuaib did for Moses.

7. Generosity and Fulfilling a Promise

Moses agreed to work for Shuaib for at least eight years, but Moses completed a total of ten years of labor. Moses was generous in his service to Shuaib, just as Shuaib had been generous to him. This is the nature of the generous. Treat others only in the best of ways, and be generous to those with whom you deal, for these are characteristics of the prophets.

8. Qualities of a Worker

The statement of Shuaib's daughter to her father was quite wise, "the best man you can hire is someone who is strong, trustworthy.'" [49] Whoever manages his or her own business should seek out employees who are strong, motivated, and have a sense of purpose. When an employee is found to be trustworthy, business and money matters can be entrusted to him or her. These workers are given more responsibility and climb to higher positions more quickly, because they have proven that they can be trusted. Employers do not have to worry about them wasting paid time on the phone or caring for personal matters during work. These workers are the ones who are always aware that God is watching, and that it is not acceptable to waste time while the employer is still paying.

9. Supplication Eases Hardship

As Moses experienced his difficulty, he needed a way to set things right, a way that was always at hand and that could immediately reach God. Supplication was just that. Use it in every situation, for it is one of the most useful tools.

---

[49] [Al-Qasas:26]

"I did not create the Jinns and the human beings except for the purpose that they should worship Me. I do not want any sustenance from them, nor do I want them to feed Me. In fact, God is the All-Sustainer, Possessor of Power, the Strong."

[Adh-Dhariyat:56-58]

— 12 —

Arrogance, the Root of Trouble

Adam and the Beginning of Creation [50]

Long ago, God wanted to exhibit the brilliance of His names and attributes, to show His absolute power and unique wisdom, and to bring the earth to flourish. So God designed creation to witness all of these wonders.

When God created man, He established mankind as deputy, to rule the earth, one generation after the next. Man was also created to build upon and populate the earth, for the jinn did not have such capabilities. Humans were designed in the finest form, and God honored mankind by blowing into man from His divine spirit.

Before creating Adam (as), God discussed the matter

---

[50] Qisas Al-Anbiyaa', pg. 5-10, by Ismail Ibn Kathir.

with the angels, "When your Lord said to the angels, 'I am going to create a deputy on the earth!'" [51]

The angels asked about this new creation. "They said, 'Will You create there one who will spread disorder on the earth and cause bloodshed, while we proclaim Your purity, along with Your praise, and sanctify Your name?' He said, 'Certainly, I know what you know not.'" [52]

The angels posed this question to God only to seek further explanation, not out of objection. Angels never disobey God, for "They fear their Lord above them and do as they are commanded." [53] The angels had witnessed the jinn corrupting the earth, so they wondered whether humans might wreak havoc on the earth just as the jinn had before. They also worried whether they had fallen short in their worship and reverence of God, so that He might be creating humans to replace them in worshipping Him. But God had great wisdom in why He was creating man, which the angels did not know.

To create Adam, God used a handful of dirt containing portions from all of its varieties on the earth. For this reason, humans are as diverse as the handful of soil from which they were created; all have different colors, attributes, and temperaments, based on the composition of their individual clay. God mentions this, "Indeed We created man from a ringing clay made of decayed mud." [54] He combined the dirt with water and to make a muddy clay. God then formed the clay into a hollow statue and let it dry and darken in color until man was like dried pottery. Adam, the first man, was shaped to have the height of sixty cubits (thirty meters or

---

[51] [Al-Baqara:30]

[52] [Al-Baqara:30]

[53] [An-Nahl:50]

[54] [Al-Hijr:26]

ninety feet). [55]

It was on a Friday that God created Adam, during the final hours of the day. God blew the spirit into Adam, and then He ordered the angels to bow down to Adam. They all bowed down except for the Devil. Previously, the Devil had been one of the righteous jinn, so God had elevated him to the status of the angels. But now, due to his defiance, he quickly fell in status. After all, God was only ordering them to bow to Adam to respect and honor him, not to worship him.

God questioned the Devil. "God said, 'What has prevented you from prostrating when I ordered you?' He said, 'I am better than him. You have created me of fire, and created him of clay.'" [56]

When God saw the Devil's arrogance and defiance, He ordered punishment. "He said, 'Then, get you down from here, it is not for you to show arrogance here. So, get out. You are one of the degraded.' He said, 'Then give me respite until a day when all will be resurrected.' He (God) said, 'You are granted respite.' He said, 'Now that You have led me astray, I will certainly sit for them (in ambush) on Your straight path. Then I will come upon them from their front side and from their behind, and from their right and from their left. You will not find most of them grateful.' He (God) said, 'Get out of here, condemned, rejected. Indeed, whosoever will follow you from among them, I will fill Hell with all of you together.'" [57]

As for the angels, God wanted to show them the greatness of man as His best creation, "And He taught Adam the names, all of them; then presented them before the angels, and said,

---

[55] Sahih, narrated by Muslim, hadith no. 1482.

[56] [Al-Araf:12]

[57] [Al-Araf:13-18]

'Tell Me their names, if you are right.'" [58] God mentions the word "truthful" because when the angels had learned that God was going to create a new creature, secretly among themselves they said, "'God will never create anything more noble in His eyes than us, nor more knowledgeable.'" [59]

So when God created Adam, who was indeed more knowledgeable and noble, the angels realized their limitations. The Quran tells us, "They said, 'To You belongs all purity! We have no knowledge except what You have given us. Surely, You alone are the All-Knowing, All-Wise.' He said, 'O Adam, tell them the names of all these.' When he told them their names, God said, 'Did I not tell you that I know the secrets of the skies and of the earth, and that I know what you disclose and what you conceal?'" [60] This was to remind them that God was well aware of what the angels had said in secret.

So Adam remained in Paradise with the angels for the time, where he enjoyed its countless blessings and incredible delights.

---

[58] [Al-Baqara:31]

[59] [Tafsir Jalalayn]

[60] [Al-Baqara:32-33]

Lessons Learned:

1. The Purpose of Creation

God created mankind for a number of reasons: to inhabit the earth, to cultivate the land, to pass down human progress through generations, and to display the magnificence of God's awesome power through His mercy, wisdom, and might. Man should not live on the earth like any other animal or creature. Rather, it is incumbent upon all of humanity to use God's blessings, such as human intellect, to work not only for themselves, but for the greater good of the community. Build, work, solve, be ever-grateful, and pass down individual abilities to the next generation, so that every person may fulfill the purpose for which God created humanity.

2. God's Love for the Angels

God is certainly capable of creating mankind without consulting the angels, but out of His kindness, He honored the angels by discussing the matter with them first. It has been said, "Whoever consults does not fail." Be among those who seek the insight of wise people by asking their advice for important matters. Even God discussed His plan with the angels, and He was certainly not in need of doing so. Remember that big decisions should never be made alone. Do not allow arrogance and weakness to diminish the importance of asking the opinion of others.

3. The Angels' Love for God

One way in which angels show their love to God is by doing everything that He orders them to do, never disobeying Him. But the angels contemplated and asked whether God's newest creation would cause trouble on Earth, just as the jinn had before. In addition, the angels did not simply wonder if God wanted a new creation, but their concern was that He may be creating man to replace them because their own worship of God was inadequate. If angels worry that their worship is deficient, how should people feel about their devotion of God?

4. Creation and Human Nature

God created Adam from a collection of the earth's various soils. Soil can be dry, soft, loose, strong, fertile, stiff, moist, or rough, among other characteristics. People have the same qualities as soil, for some people are tough by nature, while others are tender. Some have a soft demeanor, while others have dry personalities. Therefore, humans are naturally diverse by their very essence. Do not expect people to change their innate behavior, for humans cannot change how they were created. Rather, help people change in a way that compliments their inherent nature and improves the soil.

5. The Penalty of Disobeying God's Orders

God commanded the angels to bow down to Adam out of honor, and the angels did so without question. Among the angels was the Devil, who had been honored before by being elevated to the rank of the angels. But the Devil disobeyed God's command, became conceited, and degraded Adam. When God questioned his disobedience, he said, "'I am better than him. You have created me of fire, and created him of clay.'" [61]

The same behavior can be seen today. When a supervisor gives a new employee an important project,

---

[61] [Al-Araf:12]

a senior employee will often feel jealous and cheated out of the project. He begins to justify his feelings. He will likely think, "I am better than the new hire, more qualified, and I have been at the supervisor's service for years." Do not imitate the Devil's behavior in such a scenario. Instead, follow the orders that were given, accept that the situation is for the better, and have a good opinion of others who probably do have good reason for their decisions.

6. The Arrogant and Disobedient Become God's Enemy

The Devil disobeyed God and refused to bow down to Adam. This by itself was a sin that could have been forgiven. But the Devil became arrogant and said, "'I am better than him. You have created me of fire, and created him of clay.'" [62] This arrogance earned God's anger, so God banned him from Paradise. Even then, the Devil insisted upon his defiance and would not apologize or seek God's forgiveness. Rather, he held firmly to his position of rebellion and disobedience. He even asked God to lengthen his life so that he could persist in his wrongs. From that time forward, the Devil devoted himself to misguiding whomever obeyed him from the descendants of Adam. But the Devil taught a powerful lesson. No matter how large a sin might be, it can be forgiven if one seeks forgiveness and sincerely repents. And no matter how small a sin might be, persisting in it can lead one to perish forever.

7. The Way of the Devil

Watch for the Devil's ways to tempt people, for he has many different methods that are not always noticeable. For example, instead of whispering in a person's ear to avoid prayer, the Devil might remind a person of work

---

[62] [Al-Araf:12]

piling up, using such a distraction to make a person forget to pray. In addition, the Devil sometimes leads people to justify their foul behavior, such as speaking harshly or disobeying parents. Sometimes the Devil likes to make a person hesitate after deciding to do something good, like donating money to charity. This is when the Devil reminds people of their financial obligations, until this hesitation makes them decide not to give. Be aware of the Devil's many ways, ignore his whispers, and seek God's refuge from him.

8. Advance Through Knowledge

Certainly God wanted to illustrate to the angels that He honored Adam because of the knowledge He had given him, stating, "And He taught Adam the names, all of them." [63] Nations advance through knowledge and understanding, and when these important elements are neglected, nations decline. Strive to always be among those who learn and teach others. Never forget the honor man was given because of knowledge. In seeking knowledge, individuals benefit themselves and the greater community at large.

9. He Knows the Treachery of the Eyes and Whatever Is Conceal by Heart [64]

The angels forgot that God was always observing them when they spoke to one another. Out of their high opinion of God, they remarked that they would surely remain greater and more noble than mankind. They forgot that God watches everyone and is aware of everything, not just outwardly, but even the most secret of thoughts and feelings. Know that God is always present, so do not disobey Him in outward deeds, or even by inward thoughts and feelings.

---

[63] [Al-Baqara:31]
[64] [Ghafir:19]

"God created the angels with intelligence but without desires, and He created beasts with desires but without intelligence. God created man to have both intelligence and desire. Whoever has intelligence that rules over his desires is joined with the angels. And whoever lets his desires rule his intelligence is joined with the beasts."

Early Muslim Salaf

— 13 —

The First Trial

Adam and the Descent to Earth [65]

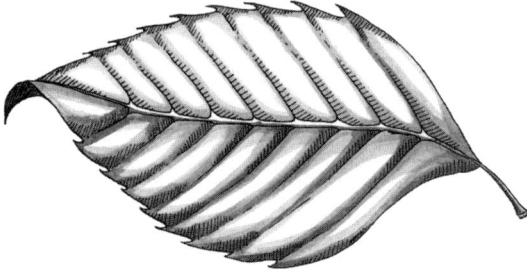

For a time, Adam (as) dwelled in Paradise, where he enjoyed its many wonders. But beside the company of the angels, Adam was alone. After a while, Adam grew lonely and restless. One night, as Adam was resting, God took one of his ribs from his left side and formed it into Eve. As God said, "O men, fear your Lord who created you from a single soul, and from it created its match." [66]

When Adam awoke, he saw the woman for the very first time, so he asked her, "Who are you?"

She replied, "I am a woman."

Adam asked her, "Why were you created?"

---

[65] Qisas Al-Anbiyaa', pg. 11-18, by Ismail Ibn Kathir.
[66] [An-Nisa:1]

"For you to live in comfort with me," she answered.

So Adam named her Eve (*Hawa'*). When Adam was asked why he chose that name, he said, "Because she was created from something living (*hayy*)." For this reason, the Prophet (pbuh) said, "Treat women well. The woman was created from a rib. The most bent part of the rib is the top part. If you try to straighten it, you will break it. If you leave it, it remains bent. So treat women well." [67] Eve was the most beautiful woman who would ever be created.

God instructed Adam, "'O Adam, dwell, you and your wife, in Paradise, and eat from wherever you like, but do not go near this tree, otherwise you shall join the transgressors.'" [68] But the Devil was lurking, and he wasted no time to begin his mission, to misguide Adam and his descendants. The Devil whispered to both Adam and Eve, tempting them to eat from the tree. God mentioned, "Then Satan whispered to them, so that he might expose to them their shame that was hidden from them; and said, 'Your Lord has not prohibited this tree for you, but to avoid your becoming angels or your becoming eternal.'" [69]

And so both Adam and Eve fell into the temptation and ate from the tree. God said, "Thus, he cast both of them down by deception. When they tasted (the fruit of) the tree, their shame was exposed to them, and they began to patch together some leaves of Paradise upon themselves, and their Lord called them, 'Did I not forbid you from that tree? Did I not tell you that Satan is your declared enemy?'" [70] Adam and Eve immediately felt terrible for the sin they had both committed. Without hesitation, they repented to God, "They said, 'Our Lord, we have wronged ourselves, and if You do not

---

[67] Narrated by Bukhari and Muslim.

[68] [Al-Araf:19]

[69] [Al-Araf:20]

[70] [Al-Araf:22]

forgive us and do not bless us with mercy, we shall, indeed, be among the losers.'" [71]

God accepted their repentance, but He said to them, "'Go down from here, all of you.'" [72] And so their punishment was to leave Paradise and its endless bliss. Adam and Eve were to live down on Earth, which in contrast was a place where they would experience troubles, exertion, and an endless need to work.

As they lived on Earth, Eve gave birth to their many children. With every pregnancy, she would deliver twins. Adam and Eve continued to have children in this pattern until she had given birth to forty pairs of twins. All of mankind descended from these children of Adam and Eve.

Once Adam came down to Earth, he began to develop the land and work hard upon it. God taught Adam various skills, such as carpentry and producing textiles, as well as different trades, like that of an ironsmith and a blacksmith. The Prophet Muhammad (pbuh) mentioned that Adam and his sons worked together to develop the earth for nine hundred and sixty years. [73]

The time eventually came when Adam's life ended, and he passed away. When he died, the angels descended to Earth, where they washed and wrapped his body in preparation to bury him. They dug a deep hole in the earth and placed Adam in it. As they covered his body up with the earth's dirt, it was established how mankind would be buried from that day forward. A short time later, Eve also passed away.

As the first man and woman to have ever lived, Adam and Eve began the cycle for all of humanity. Indeed, it is

---

[71] [Al-Araf:23]

[72] [Al-Baqara:38]

[73] Sahih hadith, Musnad of Imam Ahmed, pg. 175.

only natural for humans to have children and develop the earth, and then to pass away. These are the worldly purposes of mankind, destined to live on Earth. And no one remains forever, except God the Almighty.

Lessons Learned:

1. ## The Impact of a Wife

   Even though Adam lived in Paradise, he still felt lonely and restless. For this reason, God created a wife with whom he could live. Adam could enjoy her company, and only together could they find comfort and ease, and live in peace and tranquility. Eve would become his partner and companion, and they would handle all of the troubles of life together. Eve would bear and raise all of Adam's children, teaching and caring for them, as only a mother could. These are some of the roles of a wife, whom God first created for Adam. It is the honor of women to take on such roles, to fulfill this purpose, for which God first created them.

2. ## Loneliness Is Difficult, Even in Paradise

   Adam had every kind of delight and comfort in Paradise, but he still felt loneliness and boredom because he sought the company of another human. He needed companionship, someone to talk to and engage in discussion. This reveals much about the social needs of humanity, and the undeniable necessity of having other people with whom to engage. Choose only the best of company, because not only is it a human need, but the influence people have on one another cannot be underestimated.

3. ## The Characteristics of a Woman

   God created Eve from the rib of Adam. A rib is naturally curved, and trying to straighten one out will only break it. God reminds humanity that women are not like men. Women are much more delicate, and must be treated as such, for women are more sensitive, compassionate, and forbearing by the very nature of their creation. Do not mistreat women by placing more upon them than they should bear, or by being harsh or cruel to them. A woman is built uniquely, and she has different natural balances and cycles, causing her to have times when she is more calm, emotional, sad, moody, or irrational. This does not make her inferior, but it does make her different from a man. It is upon men to understand the basic differences in the nature of women, and to be patient and gentle during turbulent times. For this reason, the Prophet (pbuh) instructed men always to care for women and to treat women well.

4. The Wisdom of Naming "Eve" (*Hawa*)

Adam named his wife Eve ("*Hawa*"), which is derived from the same Arabic root as "*Hayy*," which means "living." A woman is delicate and sensitive like a flower, and tears are quick to run down her cheeks. Yet she is extraordinarily patient and as firm as a tree, especially in caring for her children. Her patience is heightened while bearing pregnancy, enduring childbirth, raising children, and facing the many tricky challenges along the way. She is unyielding in her generosity, and she is capable of sacrificing all that she has for those around her. This all stems from her inherent nature, as God created her different from man. Therefore, use the innate qualities given to each to improve the individual and the community. Stand up to end the use of women in demeaning ways or to promote corruption, for God has created her as a much more honorable creature.

5. Trials and Forgetfulness

God provided Adam and Eve with general rules for living in Paradise. God allowed them to eat anything they wanted, but He prohibited them from just one tree. God did so only to test them. Adam and Eve followed the rules for a while, until they overlooked the promise they had made to God. The Devil took advantage of the situation. He found his chance to whisper in their ears, telling them that eating from such a tree would make them into angels, and that this would allow them to stay in Paradise forever. They listened to him, ate from the tree, and disobeyed God. This is one of the Devil's tactics, to tempt people into acts of disobedience. He makes bad deeds feel trivial, and He takes advantage of times when a person has become distant from God. Remember that the Devil makes people forget God, and he only deludes them. So know his tricks, and do not walk into his traps. Doing so only brings about regrets later.

6. Disobedience and Punishment

When Adam and Eve ate from the tree and disobeyed their Lord, the punishment came immediately. Their clothing was torn off of their bodies, and they stood before God, embarrassed. They quickly took leaves off of the branches of the trees in Paradise to cover themselves. Modesty and covering up the body are instinctive to humans, not nakedness, despite what secular society tries to make people believe. Know that when God sends His punishment immediately after a sin is committed, it is only proof that God loves that person, for it is a reminder to return swiftly to God and repent.

7. Disobedience and Quick Repentance

As soon as Adam and Eve realized their mistakes, they repented to God and asked for His forgiveness. They began by praising God, and then they asked God for forgiveness. Adam and Eve took responsibility for their sins, and "They said, "Our Lord, we have wronged ourselves, and if You do not forgive us and do not bless us with mercy, we shall, indeed, be among the losers.'" [74] Here we see the big difference between the Devil and Adam. Both of them had sinned, but the Devil persisted in his sins and was arrogant. Therefore, he was given an eternal punishment. But Adam and Eve recognized their mistake, felt bad about it, and sincerely turned to God for forgiveness. Adam and Eve were forgiven for their sins, just as every sin can be forgiven, as long as there is sincere repentance following it.

8. Learning from Punishment

God punished Adam and Eve and expelled them from Paradise to live on Earth. But God did not abandon them on Earth, for He taught them many trades, and He gave them the opportunity to discover their own capabilities. When giving a punishment, it is very important to give the reason for the punishment, and to offer different solutions for the person to get back on track. Teach and guide others in the process, because the greater purpose should be to improve one another, not to seek revenge.

9. Death Is Inevitable, Even after a Long Life

No matter how much people accomplish, or how long they live, death will still come. Even Adam, who witnessed the birth of his eighty children and lived to the ripe old age of nine hundred and sixty years, still faced death. His wife and kids could not delay his inevitable fate, and once he passed away, he took nothing with him other than his righteous deeds. Be among those who plan for what comes after death. Do not focus all of one's efforts merely on worldly gains, for it will all come to an end.

---

[74] [Al-Araf:23]

"Indeed man is created weak in courage, very upset when touched by evil, and very niggard when visited by good (fortune), except the performers of prayer, who are regular in their prayer, and those in whose riches there is a specified right for the one who asks and the one who is deprived, and those who believe in the Day of Judgment as true, and those who are fearful of the torment of their Lord. Indeed the torment of their Lord is not something to be fearless from."

[Al-Maarij:19-28]

— 14 —

The Importance of Giving Charity (Zakah)

Abu Hurairah and the Devil [75]

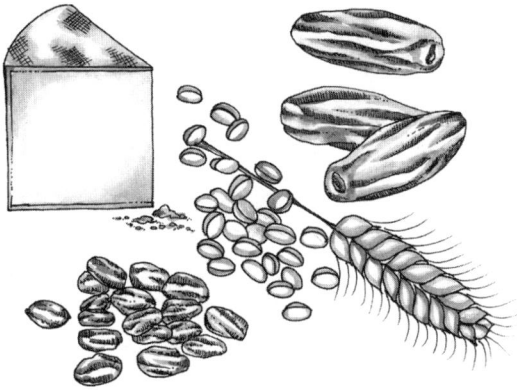

By the end of the holy month of Ramadan, it is an Islamic requirement to pay a special charity, called *Zakah*. Giving money to this form of charity during the holy month is a token of thankfulness to God for enabling Muslims to perform and complete their religious duties during the holy month. This unique charity is indeed blessed, for it purifies from sins the one who gives it. It also makes it possible for the poor and needy to celebrate the holiday of *Eid*, following Ramadan, with joy and dignity.

One year, the Prophet Muhammad (pbuh) assigned Abu Hurairah (ra) to be in charge of guarding the warehouse where the Muslims stored the donated food collected for *Zakah*. The food would be stored there until it was time to

---

[75] Hadith of the Prophet Muhammad (pbuh), related by Abu Hurairah, narrated by Bukhari.

distribute it among the needy.

One night, a man snuck in to steal from the collected goods. Abu Hurairah saw the thief and caught him. He reprimanded him and said, "By God, I will take you to the Prophet (pbuh)!"

The man pleaded, "Please! I am merely a poor man in need. I have children, and I am in desperate need of this charity." Abu Hurairah felt sympathy for the man and his sad condition, so he decided to let the man go.

The next day, the Prophet (pbuh) asked, "Oh, Abu Hurairah, what did your prisoner do yesterday?"

Abu Hurairah replied, "He told me about his desperate need and his poor children, so I had mercy on him, and I let him go."

The Prophet (pbuh) asserted, "But he did indeed lie, and he will return."

Abu Hurairah knew that the man would surely return, because the Prophet (pbuh) had mentioned it, and he only spoke the truth.

Sure enough, that evening, the man returned and secretly entered into the warehouse. Once again, he attempted to steal from the reserves of the Muslims. Abu Hurairah swiftly grabbed the man and told him, "I will be taking you to the Prophet (pbuh) to deal with you for sure!"

The man begged Abu Hurairah, saying, "Please leave me, for I am desperately poor, and I have children. Let me be, and I promise I will never return." Compassion flooded Abu Hurairah's heart for the poor man. For a second time, he let the man go free.

The next morning, the Prophet (pbuh) asked, "Oh, Abu Hurairah, what did your prisoner do yesterday?"

"Oh Prophet of God, he told me that he was in desperate need and that he had poor children, so I had mercy on him and set him free," explained Abu Hurairah.

"He has lied to you, and he will be back," the Prophet (pbuh) insisted.

For the third time, Abu Hurairah was on the lookout for the man, determined this time not to pardon the thief. The man secretly entered the warehouse to steal food for a third time. But this time, Abu Hurairah caught the man and said to him, as he held him tight, "I will be taking you to the Prophet (pbuh), for this is the third and last time you have promised not to return, and yet you have!"

Instead of pleading with Abu Hurairah to set him free, this time the man said, "Leave me, and I will teach you some words that will be of much benefit to you before God."

"And what might these words be?" Abu Huriarah asked, as his curiosity set in.

"As you lay in your bed at night, recite the verse of the Quran called *Ayat Al-Kursi* from beginning to end, 'God: There is no God but He, the Living, the All-Sustaining. Neither dozing overtakes Him nor sleep. To Him belongs all that is in the heavens and all that is on the earth. Who can intercede with Him without His permission? He knows what is before them and what is behind them; while they encompass nothing of His knowledge, except what He wills. His *Kursiyy* (Chair) extends to the heavens and to the earth, and it does not weary Him to look after them. He is the All-High, the Supreme.' [76] By doing so, you will remain in God's

---

[76] [Al-Baqara:255]

protection all night, and the Devil cannot come near you until the morning," the man claimed.

So Abu Hurairah fulfilled his part of the agreement and let the man go.

The next morning, the Prophet (pbuh) asked Abu Hurairah one last time, "What did your prisoner do yesterday?"

Abu Hurairah explained, "Dear Prophet (pbuh), the man claimed that he could teach me wise words that would benefit me greatly before God. Once he shared them with me, I had to let him go."

"What were they?" the Prophet asked.

"When lying down to go to sleep, I should recite the verse *Ayat Al-Kursi* from beginning to end. He told me that by doing so, God would continue to protect me throughout the night, and the Devil could not come near me until I awoke in the morning.

"He spoke the truth, but he also lied," The Prophet (pbuh) declared, "Do you know who you have been speaking to, Oh Abu Hurairah, for the past three nights?"

"No," replied Abu Hurairah.

"Indeed, it was Satan," revealed the Prophet (pbuh).

Lessons Learned:

1. The Importance of Giving Charity (*Zakah*)

God has given the poor the right to a portion of the wealth of those who possess it by making the charity of *Zakah* an obligation upon every financially able Muslim. Not only do such Muslims have to pay *Zakat Al-Fitr* by the end of Ramadan, but they must also pay *Zakat Al-Maal*.

Zakat Al-Maal is owed in the amount of two and one-half percent of any excess, untouched wealth, carried over from one year to the next, above a set minimum amount. This becomes a consistent, tangible reminder from God that one's wealth is merely a trust from Him, a test to see whether it will be spent for the sake of God, as it was entrusted. A portion of one's wealth should be spent in a way that pleases God, such as to provide for those less fortunate, to promote noble advancements, or to support causes that benefit humanity. When one considers the steep percentage, usually ranging between twenty and fifty percent, that everyone willingly pays in taxes in most secular nation, in comparison, the amount God has required is very minimal. This obligation should be seen as an honor, and not a burden, for the wealthy. There is no cheating or ignoring the orders of God, and being ungrateful can anger God and deplete the blessings in all of one's wealth. Instead, give generously, and receive an abundant amount of reward for helping those in need.

2. The Charity of Ramadan

The charity due by the end of Ramadan, *Zakat Al-Fitr*, is a duty upon every Muslim to feed a hungry person once a year. Traditionally, during the Prophet's time,

Zakat Al-Fitr was paid in the form of food, such as barley, dates, raisins, dried cheese, and other dried goods. Nowadays, Muslims may pay in food, or its cash equivalent, depending on whichever is more accessible to the poor. This type of *Zakat* is usually collected locally and distributed the morning of *Eid*, the holiday that commences Ramadan. In addition, *Zakat Al-Maal* is often given out during Ramadan, simply because it is an easy time of year to remember this yearly obligation. It is also a chance to multiply the reward for this type of *Zakah* by giving it during this blessed month, when all good deeds are multiplied. From the story, it was not specified which of the two types of *Zakah* was being guarded by Abu Hurairah, but it was clear that *Zakah* was sometimes stored throughout Ramadan, to be given out at the end of the month.

3. Taking Food Without Permission

Abu Hurairah caught the man who was stealing food, so he told him that he was taking the matter to the Prophet (pbuh). At this point, the man fabricated a story about his drastic financial situation and impoverished children. Only then did Abu Hurairah pardon the man and dismiss the matter, without bringing it before the Prophet (pbuh), so that the man would not have to face the charges for theft. This is a powerful portrayal of forgiveness that is found in the religion of Islam, remarkable for its extra mercy and leniency toward the poor and needy. Abu Hurairah displayed how the poor and needy needed to be treated with greater special care, not less. Islam teaches believers to be kind and merciful with the less fortunate and those with young, needy children.

4. Wisdom Is the Lost Property of the Believer

Satan knew what would be of benefit to the believer. He advised Abu Hurairah, but he did not consider taking his own advice. Take valuable lessons from wherever they may be, for even Satan can teach an important lesson. Also, there is even something to be learned from those who do not take their own advice. Be humble and accept advice. Wisdom is the lost property of the believer, so wherever a believer finds it, he or she should take it.

5. Satan Lies and Changes Form

Satan is the Devil, who is from the jinn, and the jinn are able to change their form. Therefore, it is possible for humans to see him. God mentions this: "Indeed, he sees you – he and his company – from where you do not see them." [77] Abu Hurairah learned that Satan lied, stole, and took the food of the needy. Watch out for Satan, and beware of his whispers and his tricky ways. He was able to fool Abu Hurairah three times, and he was even granted Abu Hurairah's pardon repeatedly. What might Satan do today, and how many times does one fall into his deception and traps?

6. Accepting Excuses and Hiding Faults

Abu Hurairah excused the man because he believed that he was telling the truth, so Abu Hurairah pardoned him and let him go free. It is always best to be among those who are quick to forgive, pardon, excuse, and hide the faults of others. After all, they might be guided back to doing only good.

7. The Protection of Reading the Verse *Ayat Al-Kursi*

When Abu Hurairah mentioned the advice of the man to the Prophet (pbuh), that he should read the

---

[77] [Al-Araf:27]

verse nightly, he responded, "He spoke the truth, but he also lied." This illustrates the importance of this powerful verse from the Quran. *Ayat Al-Kursi* will indeed protect the one who reads it at night, and it will keep Satan away, so read the verse regularly to be among those protected by God, and be far from Satan.

"Oh people, Islam is truly a solid wall and a secure door. The wall of Islam is truth, and the door is justice, and Islam will continue to be solid as long as its authority is strong. Its strength does not come from fighting with a sword or lashing with a whip, but rather from ruling with truth, and practicing justice."

Sa'eed Ibn Suwaid, Lecture in Homs, Syria

— 15 —
The Recipients of Charity (Zakah)
The Rule of 'Umar Ibn Abdul-Aziz [78]

During the time of the Muslim caliph 'Umar ibn Abdul-Aziz, who ruled for about thirty months, the people witnessed a unique time of prosperity for the Muslims. Throughout the land, there was an abundance of justice, righteousness, safety, and tranquility that they had never before experienced. Indeed, people lived with dignity, strength, and honor like never before.

At one point in time, the caliph 'Umar was surprised by the concerns and complaints coming from the capitals of various parts of the empire, which included Egypt, Syria, Iraq, and various parts of Asia and Africa. But the common problem was a rather peculiar one. They complained that there was a shortage of space to store the extra money and goods collected for *Zakah* charity. They had already

[78] Tawjihaat al-Mu'assasah al-Zakawiyyah fi Tawzi' al-Zakah ("Allocations of Zakah Oraganizations in Zakah Distribution") by Dr. Ala'al-Din Al-Za'tari

103

distributed the charity to all those who qualified for it, yet there was still too much left over beyond what the treasury storehouses could fill. They posed the dilemma to the caliph in order to solve the problem.

'Umar Ibn Abdul-Aziz thought about the problem, and he decided that the extra money could go to equip the armies with weaponry and materials. He sent his message to all of the nations, and the leaders spent from the treasury on all of the armies' needs. But they returned with the same complaint, that there was still too much in excess.

The caliph contemplated the issue some more, and he sent out a second solution. An announcement was to be made throughout the neighborhoods in all of the lands. They were to announce that whoever worked in the state but did not own a home should be built a home from the funds in the treasury. In addition, whoever did not have a means of transportation should be given one, purchased by the Muslim treasury. Also, whoever had a debt that they could not pay, the debt would be paid off by the treasury. In addition, whoever wished to get married, but could not afford to do so, would have their expenses covered by the Muslim treasury.

The leaders and treasurers carried out the caliph's instructions. They went through their lands announcing, purchasing, and distributing the needs and amenities of the people from the funds in their treasuries.

'Umar thought that the matter was resolved until he received yet the same concern once again. Even now, after all of these needs of the people were met, there was still more money than could fill the treasury storehouses.

So the caliph sent back another resolution. Now money was to be given to those in need among the Jews and the

Christians to cover their needs, so that even their debts would be paid off from the Muslim treasury. The leaders and treasurers went to work distributing all of the money they could to all of those who needed it, as the caliph had instructed.

Yet again, the same complaint returned to 'Umar. There was simply too much money left over, more funds than could even be stored.

"What more can I do?" he wondered. 'Umar ibn Abdul-Aziz thought for awhile before making a decision. Finally he said, "This is only from the bounty of God, and He gives it to whomever He pleases. Buy seeds and disperse them on the mountaintops for the birds to eat until the birds are full, so that no one may ever say that even a bird went hungry in the land of the Muslims."

His order was carried out, and so this was how people lived in prosperity during the time of this fair and noble caliph, who spread goodness throughout the land.

Lessons Learned:

1. Ruling with Justice Brings About Blessings

'Umar Ibn Abdul-Aziz ruled with justice in the empire, and this brought God's blessings to the land. He feared God in his rule, and he held himself accountable before anyone else. From other historical sources, it has been recorded that 'Umar Ibn Abdul-Aziz and his wife also donated to the treasury from their own personal wealth when he first began his rule. Out of his fairness, he cut unnecessary and excessive expenses throughout the empire, and he even reduced pay for many positions of leadership. Thus he was fair to himself and to his staff, so the people in the land followed in his footsteps and were also fair. Remember always to be a positive example for others, and do not try to preach what is not first put into practice.

2. *Zakah* Charity and Its Distribution

During the rule of this caliph, the zakah charity was distributed to those who qualified for it. God enumerated them: "The *Sadaqat* (prescribed alms) are (meant) only to be given to the poor, the needy, to those employed to collect them, to those whose hearts are to be won, in the cause of the slaves and those encumbered with debt, in the way of God and to a wayfarer. This is an obligation prescribed by God. God is All-Knowing, Wise." [79] After giving out charity to these various categories, the treasury was still overfilled. This can only mean that the recipients were not taking advantage of public funds by taking extra money. Rather, the people were fair in taking only as much as they needed so that others could do the same, and so that all of society would benefit. Only forward-

---

[79] [Al-Tawba:60]

thinking people of upright character would dismiss their personal greed and selfish motives to remember the greater community.

3. **Priorities of the Muslim Empire**

The caliph made the first priority, after taking care of the needy, to furnish the needs of the army in order to protect the empire. He understood that if a nation's army is strong, its enemies will be intimidated, and its citizens will feel secure. Because they will not be worried about their safety, the people can instead focus on innovative advancements and the development of the country. Advanced nations are those that make sure their citizens feel safe, and treat their people fairly.

4. **God Helps the Leaders Who Work Hard for Their Citizens**

The caliph 'Umar made sure that the poor and needy were taken care of, the armies were equipped, the young adults were able to get married, and those financially struggling were freed of debts and given homes and transportation. He thought deeply about all of the different financial needs of the different nations and their citizens, and he addressed all of them. As the Prophet (pbuh) said, "A Muslim is the brother of another Muslim, so he should not oppress him, nor should he hand him over to his enemy. Whoever fulfilled the needs of his brother, God will fulfill his needs; whoever brought his Muslim brother out of distress, God will bring him out of distress on the Day of Resurrection; and whoever concealed the faults of a Muslim, God will conceal his faults on the Day of Resurrection." [80]

---

[80] Narrated by Ahmed, Bukhari, and Muslim.

5. Equal Rights Under Islamic Rule

The caliph was fair and equal in his distribution of funds among the Muslims (who had paid the *zakah* charity), and among those of other faiths who did not contribute to these funds, but lived in the Muslim lands. Still, he took care of the poor and covered their needs, just as he had done for the Muslims. The caliph understood that as the leader, he had the grave responsibility of taking care of all of the citizens of the empire, regardless of their religion. He knew better than to treat those of other faiths differently, as God said, "Say (O, Muslims): 'We believe in God, and in what has been revealed to us, and in what has been revealed to *Ibrahim* (Abraham), *Isma'il* (Ishmael), *Ishaq* (Isaac), *Ya'qub* (Jacob) and his children, and in what has been given to *Musa* (Moses) and *'Isa* (Jesus) and what has been given to the prophets from their Lord: We make no difference between any of them, and to Him we submit ourselves.'" [81] For this reason, it is always important to treat people of all faiths kindly and fairly. Do not differentiate among people according to religion, but rather see everyone as brothers and sisters in humanity.

6. Good Care of Animals

The caliph 'Umar was extremely sensitive regarding the magnitude of his responsibility. In fact, it reached the point where he feared that if even the birds were not fed properly, he would be held responsible for their hunger before his Lord. If only the nations and governments of the world today could follow this caliph's example, to ask themselves, indeed, for whose care they will be held accountable. Only rulers worthy of their positions feel the weight of their responsibility, and their actions prove that they take themselves to

---

[81] [Al-Baqara:136]

account before anyone else. They should certainly do so before their Lord takes them to account.

7. All Is from the Bounty of God: He Gives to Whomever He Pleases

'Umar did not take the credit for all of the good that his acts of justice and wisdom caused to spread throughout the Muslim world. Instead, he recognized that the blessings came from God alone. He understood that had God not paved the way, none of what he was able to accomplish would have been possible. Never forget that everything good in life is purely out of God's generosity. Thank and praise God often, and learn to really mean it from the bottom of one's heart. Indeed, it is only out of His extraordinary generosity that anyone is ever able to achieve his or her accomplishments.

Other Titles by the Author

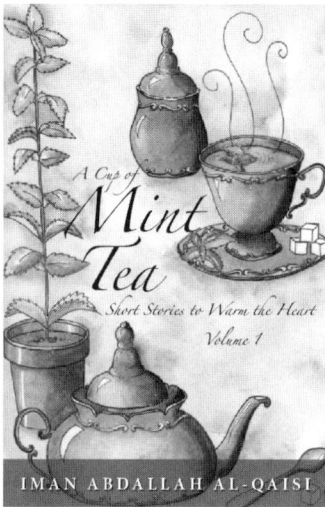

A CUP OF MINT TEA
Volume 1
Short Stories to Warm the Heart

*The Virtues of Reading Quran * Live by the Verses of the Quran * Quran is Light * Quran for Healing * The Importance of Prayer (Martyrdom of 'Umar) * The Importance of Perfecting Prayer * The Importance of Friday Prayer * Reverence in Prayer * The Importance of Fajr Prayer * The Importance of Praying with a Group * Midnight Prayers * Honesty Is Your Protector * Being Truthful with the Prophet (PBUH) * The Price of Honesty * God is the Creator (Abu Hanifa and the Athiest)*

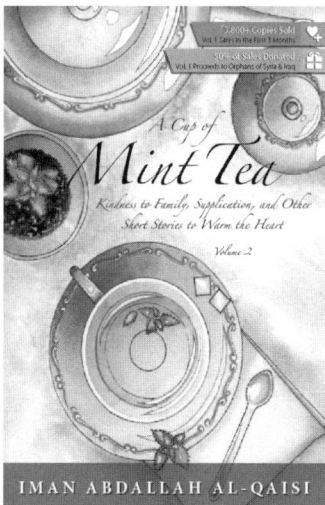

A CUP OF MINT TEA
Volume 2
Kindness to Family, Supplication, and Other Short Stories to Warm the Heart

*The Act of Sincerity * How Can I Be Good to My Mother? * Kindness to Parents * Dear to God, Dutiful to Parents * God Is the Merciful * God, the Giver of Life * Fasting and Higher Consciousness * The Reward for the Fasting * Supplication Is the Heart of Worship * Supplication: Relief from Distress * The Acceptance of True Supplication * The Etiquette of Eating * The Food of the Generous Is Medicine * Charity Begins at Home * The Fruits of Maintaining Bonds of Kinship*